MOMMA
I
SHOULD
HAVE
LISTENED

A Voice of Pain and Power

TOSHA SMITH MILLS
Contributions by BJ SMITH

Cover Design: Ashley Delaney
Editor: Nikki Toups
Author's Photograph by Christopher Horne Photography
ISBN: 1548213985
ISBN-13: 978-1548213985

"Each of us is more than the worst thing we've ever done."

--Bryan Stevenson, Just Mercy: A Story of Justice and Redemption

"Owning our story can be hard, but not really as difficult as spending our lives running from it. Embracing our vulnerability is risky but not nearly as dangerous as giving up on love and belonging and joy- the experiences that make us the most vulnerable. Only when we are brave enough to explore the darkness will we discover the infinite power of our light."

--Brene Brown, The Gifts of Imperfection

DEDICATIONS

My mother, *Fannyé White Strickland*, who allowed me to fail miserably as a teenager; who allowed me to make countless mistakes; who allowed me to make choices that she knew would be detrimental; who gave me a roof over my head, unconditional love, lessons that needed to be learned, and the no's that she knew would turn into know-hows. For all of this, I am extremely grateful. Mom, I love you from this earth to you in Heaven.

My grandmother, *Mathilda White Claiborne,* who always provided a shoulder to cry on; who was in the delivery room when my first son was born through when my last son was born; and who was there the day my eldest son received that fateful sentence that neither of us will ever forget. Thank you for always being there for me. I love you.

My grandmother, *Sadie Smith,* who always has my back and been my rock. Thank you for driving fifteen miles a day to watch my son so I could finish school. I could not have done half of this and wouldn't be the person I am today without you. When I needed someone the most, you were there for me. I love you.

To every incarcerated human whether in the mind or in a cell, every parentless child, every childless parent, and every parent or child that has endured pain and suffering at the expense of someone else, I am deeply sorry.

FOREWORD

I have known Tosha Smith Mills for a little over half a decade now. I first met her when we worked together at a law firm in New Orleans, and I learned quickly that she was sharp, hard-working, and ambitious. I knew that she was a talent agent, and over the years had thrilled at seeing her alongside her clients at red carpet premieres. Little did I know that shortly before I met her, she had experienced a parent's worst nightmare, short of the death of a child.

When Tosha called to ask me to write this foreword, I had no idea of the unimaginable pain she had been harboring for the entire time I had known her: her eldest son, serving a forty-year sentence for a crime he had committed as a teenager. Frankly, I was surprised, because I had always known her to be so full of positivity and encouragement. When she told me her story and asked me to write this foreword, I agreed without hesitation, because I knew that the advice she would dispense would come from a person who has experienced deep loss and pain, yet who has not allowed that pain to control her life, instead using it as a kind of fuel to drive her many accomplishments.

My work as an attorney involves representing children in the foster care system in the metropolitan New Orleans area. Though I do not handle juvenile delinquency cases, many of my clients are involved in parallel criminal proceedings. My experience with these kids gives me great compassion for them. Science tells us that impulse control in the human brain is not cemented until well into a person's early-to-mid-twenties. Take an adolescent brain, introduce peer pressure, drugs, abuse and violence, or any combination thereof, and you have a recipe for mistakes being made – even grave mistakes with grave consequences. Mistakes they are, and too often our society has little compassion or mercy for young people, especially young men of color. I often marvel at how easily people forget the mistakes of their own youths. May Tosha's story, and her son's, remind us all of our own fallibility, and our own need for mercy and redemption.

Jesse S. George, Esquire

ACKNOWLEDGEMENTS

I FINISHED! I DID IT! Thank you to everyone that is reading this book at this very moment. My story belongs to you. I would not have an audience if it were not for you. Your support means so much to me. I put my whole heart, soul and life in this writing and it was not easy. I cried so many days and nights, but I got through it. There are a number of exceptional people who contributed in more ways than one in the writing of this book. So many family and friends supported me during my writings, but I have a few special people to thank. If I forget anyone, I am deeply sorry.

Various times when I wanted to quit and not share my story, it was God that showed up anonymously in my life shifting my perspective from not writing to giving me vision to write something better. Thank you, God!

Thank you to the hardest working man that I know ... my husband and best friend, John. God took what was a friendship first and molded it into a great relationship. Your love and daily encouragement means the world to me. When it seems as though I am not listening, I promise you that I am. Nothing goes unnoticed. For every kiss on my forehead and every prayer that you prayed with me, I found enriched strength to keep moving forward. You are my rock and my biggest cheerleader. Without you, so many things would not have come to fruition. I forever thank you and love you.

Thank you to my other children, William (Bill), Trae, and Christopher, for being my strength through all of this. Bill, thank you for creating the concept of the cover. Something about the mother and son hands resonated with me over and over again. Christopher, thank you for reading this book fifty times over and making sure that each I was dotted and every T was crossed. You are such a perfectionist. I have learned so much from each of you throughout writing this book. Most importantly, I learned that while we are not perfect, we are perfect for each other. I love you all more than life itself.

Thank you to Christopher Horne Photography. The photo shoot in preparation for the release of the book was something I envisioned. You captured the smile that I have always felt, but was afraid to display because of the pain. When I look at the author's picture, it reinforces the happiness that I have embraced from within. You are the best photographer in the universe.

Thank you to Simone Mills, my bonus daughter through marriage. Your writing skills are impeccable, and your contribution to the heart of this book was on point. Every question that I needed an answer for, you pulled it and discovered it through my writings. You are the smartest and most respectable nineteen-year-old young lady that I know. Thank you and I love you.

Thank you to my sisters, Alvani and Staar, who have constantly reminded me of the power that I possess from within when I thought the power was limited. Our bond is unbreakable; Momma would be so proud of us. I love you.

Thank you to my only earthly living parent, Alvin Smith. We disagree, we argue, we laugh, we love; the respect that I have for you is unwavering. Thank you for being there when I need you the most. I love you, Daddy.

My God, I do not know what I would have done without you Nikki Toups. You are not only one of my best friends, but you are one of the smartest people I know. Thank you for editing this book and being one of the primary reasons that I finished this book even with your health scare. You are my rock. I love you to the moon and back.

Thank you, Lloyd Watts, my brother from another family. You were so instrumental in my life from the day we met. Thank you for reminding me of the many gifts that I have to unlock doors.

Thank you, Faith May, for being the Captain of my personal pep squad. You became that encouraging sounding board that made so much noise when I needed it the most.

Adele Tennyson, when I told you I was finished with this book, you made sure that everything I needed was there. In your words, "It must be done right or not at all." We do not talk everyday but when we do, it can last for days on end. Thank you for investing me. You are the big sister that I always wish I had.

Thank you to my Aunt Marguerite Bright White who is not just my Aunt but also my friend. I am so happy that our hearts intertwined again. Our talks and laughter on our weekly drives to our favorite spots became my therapy when I was going through severe writer's block. Thank you for your constant encouragement and listening to my cries when I discussed that this book would never get published. I love you.

Last, but not least, and with a full heart, thank you to my eldest son, Blake. Thank you for contributing to our story. You are my inspiration! We have a bond that can never be broken, not even through concrete walls. We found our voice, Blake! The love that I have for you is not only unconditional, it is immeasurable. We have a fight for injustice of time on our hands – let's get ready for war.

INTRODUCTION

SEPTEMBER 16, 2009 … the absolute worst day of my life.

At 12:58 p.m., somewhere around the world, a beautiful child was being born, a couple just got married, a death was taking place, challenges were overcome, and successes were celebrated. For me, I had just heard words that instantly changed my life beyond comprehension.

I remember the moment as if it were only yesterday. I could feel the silence of the room, the musty smell, and it felt like my heart would beat right out of my chest. Then, as if in slow motion, I heard the words and remember yelling a deafening "NO!" I was in complete and utter disbelief. This could not be real. As my eighty-two-year-old grandmother stood beside me, I clung to her with all my might. My heart felt as if it had stopped beating. My legs were suddenly numb, and my voice became inaudible. I felt powerless, weak, and shaken to the core. I had been thrown into a journey that was not part of my roadmap. Suddenly and without warning, I had been involuntarily inducted into an assembly line of parents with incarcerated children. Mommy did not feel like mommy anymore. I did not know what to feel or think. How could this be happening?

Upon writing this Introduction, my son began his seventh year of a forty-year sentence for aggravated assault with a weapon. At merely seventeen years old, my son had become the property of the Texas Penal System. Until now, I have only shared a minute fraction of what my life has been like for the past seven years. What remains constant is that our lives were forever changed that day.

For seven years, I have kept a journal of my experiences as a mother whose son is living his life behind bars. For the first five years, I hid behind a veil of embarrassment, lies, and shame. Having been very judgmental in the past, I was suddenly aware of how wrong I had been to do so. I am immensely apologetic to any parent and child who must endure the gut wrenching agony of going through such an experience. I have learned that it is my responsibility to refrain from judging another person's character by what I see in their children. I relate to others in ways I never thought possible. Like most people, I never thought it would happen to me.

With no doubt in my mind whatsoever, I knew that my children would never do anything wrong in the eyes of the law. That only happened to other children; not mine! Never say never. When I found out that my son had committed a crime, it felt impossible and surreal. Surely, it was just a nightmare and I would wake up at any second. I felt like I needed to be rescued from a burning building that had collapsed on me ten times over and, after collapsing, I had to be resuscitated when I was certain I was already dead.

Writing this book for many years, I found myself pausing frequently, because I needed it to be an authentic masterpiece. I needed every word to be candid and full of conviction. I knew that would only happen by reliving every moment, and it was imperative that I prepared for that. More significantly, I needed my words to be a barefaced description of my experience, so all parents with children experiencing life within the criminal judicial system would realize they are not alone. I needed people to know that I am here for them. I want parents and children to know that I understand the shock, pain, helplessness, and emptiness that can consume your life. It is extremely important to give you a front row seat to my experience. Ultimately, if my story can save you or your child from making the same mistakes and going through the same pain, then it has been worthwhile to expose my raw truth.

While reading this story, you may often ask, "How can such an astute and talented child, who was raised in a devoted middle-class family, be in this situation? How could he be completely aware of the consequences for such choices; yet, make them?" Throughout each chapter, my son will express himself through his own brutally honest words about how the streets, the drugs, and the peer pressure preyed on him.

My greatest aspiration is that this book empowers young men and women to resist peer pressure and to stand tall against a failing social system. Like myself, you may find yourself overcome by various emotions. Though this was not easy to write and quite painful to relive, I am proud to say I found my voice through it all. No one is born to be a criminal. No one is born to harm themselves. I am hopeful that my story, my words, and my compassion will the path of anyone thinking about destructive behavior. I implore you to open your heart and allow me to bring you through the complex experience of a mother who goes through an unexpected journey ... a journey that I would never wish upon any parent or child.

Let's be clear. This is not just a me problem; this is an equal opportunity problem.

PROLOGUE

As I was reading the finishing touches of this book, I felt so guilty inside. I damn near cried, but I've been through so much it's hard to cry these days. But I felt guilty because I wish I would have been more attentive, more understanding, attentive, more observant to the things that were transpiring around me. I guess the title of the book says it all, I wish I would have listened to my momma. It seems as if everyone knew I was making some pretty bad decisions but me, why is that? I ask myself everyday sitting in these four walls. You know what? I probably would be able to justify certain stuff; I probably can make some worthy excuses to have you believe that I was under some raw circumstances. I had a stepdad who hated my real dad so he took it out on me or since I was not his child, he showed favoritism or he was abusive physically or emotionally that kept me mentally off balance. I can sit here and give you situation after situation to justify my actions, but you know what? It does not matter.

I am my own person and I'm the one in this prison right now with no air conditioner and it is damn near 100 degrees on annual lockdown and eating two sandwiches three times a day with a Mexican guy with fifty years that I barely even know. I am the one who robbed and took people for their money with a little crew I had running in Southwest Houston. I am the only one who got caught and it was four of us and ask me how many times in nine years did I receive letter from my so called friends. One of them doing fifteen years in Louisiana which happens to be my little brother on my dad's side of the family. I received maybe three letters from the most from him. It is crazy and

District Attorney was trying to get me to turn state on them. I have to laugh to keep from crying.

I am saying all that to say this. It's not worth it. You hate school? It's a million of us fighting to go to school. We can't make parole without taking classes. You have a girlfriend or wife you are cheating on, beating her, taking advantage of her, It is a million of us looking for that same type of woman. You disrespecting MOMMA, you make her cry, you got momma crying and having chest pains, missing work to bring you back to school or court dates, that' is WEAK. Momma is the one who is going to put money on your books in prison, driving hours to visit, sending letters and birthday cards.

Do not get it mistaken, I understand, I have been in your shoes. Everything I am telling you, I been through or I am going through it; it just is not logical and does not make sense. Everything I am telling you is to better you. IF you are reading this than I assume your mom or someone that care about you asked you to read it. I assume that you still have an opportunity to dodge going to prison or have a chance to turn your life around. Take heed.

I know it is a lot of pressure out there; I know that the drugs make you feel good. I know that sometimes your parents will make you mad, but trust me, there is no hard intended; they just want the best for you.

I am twenty-six years old, got sent to prison at seventeen and I will not see parole until 2029. My cell mate has fifty years. There are men in here with sixty years all the way to one hundred and twenty nine years and they all will tell you.......It was not worth it.

We are hoping and praying that Greg Abbott, the Governor of Texas will change the laws so many of us can see daylight again; at least for me, I have a chance. Some of them would like to see their kids graduate and see their kids have kids.

It is all levels to life. You will go through a million phases. Please do not give up on yourself. I know that its hard; it will get greater later. Nothing is free in life. The harder you work , the more you will get out of the hard work that you are doing. Sometimes life will bring you down and through some unexpected changes, but as long as you are still breathing, you can get back up and you have another day to get it right.

Be a strong man. Life is short when you are living great, but it is very long when you are doing life in prison. Do not experience the latter. This is the word of advice from a talented brother who received forty years in prison for something worthless.

Love BJ

THE PAIN

"If hearts could shatter, mine just did."
ABBI GLINES, BREATHE

THE STORM

"You may know someone's face, but it does not mean you know the journey they are walking through."

-Faith May

From the beginning of 2006 until the beginning of 2009, my fear became my norm. Each time there was a knock at the door, my heartbeat quickened and panic overcame me. I could picture the coroner at the door asking me to identify my son. Each time the phone would ring, I would ignore the ring, because I was scared it was another ambush of bad news. Each light that glared in my bedroom from a passing car made my chest tighten; I had severe panic attacks as a result. The paranoia that I faced on a daily basis was more than my mind could handle. My mind was in airplane mode, and the turbulence had a distorted sound of its own. I lived in fear never knowing what would happen next to my son.

One day while sitting at the kitchen table assisting my youngest son with his homework, my phone kept ringing incessantly. Upon the fourth call ringing, I looked at the phone recognizing a Texas area code. Reluctant to answer,

I did so in case it was something important. I practically whispered, "Hello." On the other end I heard, "It's me and our son is in jail for aggravated robbery." My first instinct was annoyance by the dialogue "…our son," because when did he suddenly become "our son" since you have not been around. I responded in a very sarcastic tone, "Really? So what are you going to do for 'our son'?" He responded, "This is serious. You need to do something, and we have to hire a lawyer or something. His bond is $250,000." I responded, "There is nothing that I can do, and there is nothing that I will do. After going through this for two years, he decided to leave here and run to you. You deal with it and have a good night." Then I hung up and did not give the conversation another thought. My seventeen-year-old son, who is not old enough to vote and barely old enough to drive, was in fact old enough to be charged as an adult and was now sitting in the Harris County jail.

Four months prior, my son made the decision to move to Texas to live with his dad. Walking towards the front door, BJ's words were, "I am going to live with my dad." Upon announcing this move, the day was no different for him as the diabolical behavior, drugs, lies, and deceit had become part of his self-destructive world. For me, today was different. Looking perplexed, I mustered, "Okay son, I am now leaving you in God's hands." He replied, "That's what you do – leave me in God's hands." The streets, peer pressure, worthless friends, drugs, and a father he barely knew became his best friends, and I became his enemy. My best friend was still God and preaching, praying, and crying became my daily rituals.

The minute the door closed behind him, I cried and asked God to protect him from evil and harm. I asked God to protect my heart and make me stronger for my other three children. I needed God to hear my prayers, because I was scared and weary. I felt weak and inferior. I had been through enormous adversities; yet, each time I tried to say,

"No more," I would eventually break down and say, "Yes." Not this time. I stood tall and let my strength overcome my weakness. I was tired of fighting and feeling overwhelmed. I knew I was becoming the parent that I tried to protect him from.

Inevitably, when trouble arrived, I suddenly became my son's ally again. This time though, my actions would be far different from those he was used to receiving. I made a conscious decision to hold my son accountable for his actions. He would have to be responsible not only for what he was doing to me, but for what he was doing to himself. After two years of appalling, uncharacteristic, and intolerable behavior, I forced myself to be unemotionally attached to my son.

In hindsight, BJ was my challenging offspring with his behavior becoming troubling whenever I questioned his motive for anything out of the normal. Subtle signs of running away when he faced discipline in our home, constant pestering and disrespect toward anyone of authority, baseless threats, and unfamiliar people knocking on our door were all signs that pushed me to starting my own intervention.

I took my son to Juvenile Services believing we would receive help only to realize it would worsen the situation. After several talks with officers of the court, everything seemed to worsen. Living with him, worrying about him, rushing home after work to make sure he came home from school, and not trusting what would or could happen became daily burdens. My home was slowly and steadily becoming a living hell.

One particular evening, I came home to discover BJ was not there. I called friend after friend. I walked block after block as an attempt to find him. I drove miles and miles searching for him. There were no signs of him to be found anywhere I looked. I filed a police report and listed him as a runaway with the hope that the police would find him. As the days went by, not knowing his whereabouts was pure torture. Many nights I cried myself to sleep with my journal in one hand and the bible in the other.

I continued to say the same words over and over. "God, please help me find my son. Please save my son." I could not talk to anyone, because I was embarrassed and ashamed to admit I had no idea where my son was located. I could not call my mother, because she was dying and I refused to burden her with my problems for fear it would have shortened her life even further. I was living alone in a mental prison without a single person to console me and then the inevitable happened: my mother died.

The task of planning a funeral while grieving for both my mother and son was absolutely shattering. I was heartbroken. I lost three souls – my mom, my son, and my own.

The shame and embarrassment of my son's disappearance was demoralizing. Eventually, I received a call telling me my son had been found. He was living with his paternal aunt who I had never known. My cries for help went unnoticed. His newfound aunt blamed me for my son not going to school, because his tuition had supposedly not been paid. I yelled with exhaustion in my voice, "Excuse me ma'am, you don't even know me and clearly I don't know you. His tuition has been paid in full for the year." With each accusatory word from her, I kept trying to find reasons why this unknown person was harboring my sixteen-year-old son. The police were called, and she was warned that if she allowed my son back into her home she would be arrested for kidnapping. Did that stop her? No! I often questioned her motives for keeping him there, but there were never any answers.

Soon after my mother's funeral, my son was arrested again for being a runaway and possession of marijuana. Again, I found myself at Juvenile Services. With him, it was a vicious cycle. I would constantly bail him out, and he would be apologetic. Our home would be peaceful for a while, but unsurprisingly, it would go back to being abnormal, which was our normal. If I was lucky, things would be good for a few days or even weeks, but then, the unthinkable would happen. BJ would go missing again.

As with all things, there comes an end to the madness. That day came when BJ was picked up for the last time in New Orleans before he found himself in Texas. We were always seen before the same judge who would always be easy on him and hard on me. She would conduct a full investigation and order counseling. As if it was not embarrassing enough, the judge assigned a probation officer who I had personally known since I was young. BJ's handsome face and manipulative spirit always made the judge easy with him, but not this time.

This time, she was peculiarly harsh. She yelled, "I'm tired of you. You have been given so many chances. Do you know how many people your age wish they had the opportunities that you've had? I am locking you up in juvenile prison for thirty days, and then, at your next court appearance, I will decide what to do with you. I am going to make a determination as to whether or not I should lock you up for the rest of your juvenile life."

Frightened and fearful of what could happen, I asked a dear friend, who also is an attorney, to please defend him. Janice would write letters to him. She would go to the facility and read books with him. All she asked of him was that he be honest with her about his thoughts and feelings. At the hearing, the judge went against her better judgment and decided to release him to my custody. Sadly, it was only a matter of time before I would be sorry that she released him, because he eventually left to live with his father.

The calm and peace in my modest home returned. BJ would call me at least once a week. He would always ask how I was doing and usually asked for money. My tradition, even today, is never to go anywhere or to bed without telling my children that I love them. The call would always end with "I love you" from both of us as it always had.

As the days progressed in a positive motion and my inner pain ever so slowly subsided, I was finally able to rest peacefully. That is, until the evening I received that call from his dad that BJ had been arrested. A couple of days later, I received a call from my son. He said, "Momma, I am in trouble, and I need your help. Nobody can help me but you. Can you get the lawyers you work for to help me or get any lawyer to help me?" With every fiber of my being, I remained strong during that call. Honestly though, the reality of everything was very dark and scary. I became paralyzed with fear as I was listening to the sounds of emotional unstableness and the deep internal pain in my son's voice.

With my voice trembling and shaking I responded, "You are in Texas which is out of the jurisdiction of my legal capabilities. I am sorry son, but I cannot afford a lawyer. This is horrible. As much as I would like to sympathize with you, I cannot. I feared this day would come, and I often prayed that this would never happen; unfortunately, you made your bed, and now you have to lie in it. I love you, BJ, and will talk to you soon." This was the absolute most difficult conversation I had ever had with my son. It was brutal and broke my heart, but I knew it was the right thing to do.

This was not me turning my back on my first-born son or ignoring the issue; this was merely softening my own feelings and heartbreak, so I could once again deal with what was forthcoming. It is so painful to give up on someone that you believed was destined for greatness. As cold as it sounds, my heart had reached the end of the rope with disappointment, grief, and suffering at the hands of my son's repeated poor decisions. My first born son who I loved dearly had broken my spirit and paralyzed my ability to be compassionate, understanding, and able to fix his wrongdoings. I did not know who he was anymore. His brothers did not know who he was anymore. My son had inherited deception of the streets and this was the hardest of every reality that a parent could endure. I actually slept easier on this night knowing that he was off the street and safe.

This was a tragedy that should have never existed.

IDENTITY THEFT

"All discomfort comes from suppressing your true
identity."
-Bryant McGill

Weeks went by before I received a call from the public
defender. He asked me when could I come to Texas to meet
with him. I explained to him that I was planning on being
in Texas to visit my son in two weeks and could schedule a
meeting for that time. He penciled me in his appointment
book and told me that he wanted me to list the positive and
negative aspects of my son's life.

In my personal opinion, good public defenders were
there to help you and be your personal advocate. Not-so-
good public defenders were there to collect a paycheck
from the City Public Defenders office and hold very
minimal regard to the defendant's judicial standing. I was
praying this man was not the latter of the two.

In preparation for this meeting, I found myself crying
and feeling empathy for the first time since my son had
been locked up My imagination ran wild with images of
him using his amazing talents to perform at various venues
around the world. I wanted to know what went wrong. I
started to write down the pros and cons of my son's life to
present to the public defender. The positives, undoubtedly
to myself and to those who knew him personally,

outweighed the negatives. In making this list, I noticed something bigger was happening. Why did it seem like I had been gradually losing my child through the many changes of our lives?

Looking over the list, I questioned whether or not my son even knew his own identity. He was completely lost with no direction and seemed to be at war with himself. Was he depressed and was I just not aware of an identity crisis that he was experiencing? Since I received the call that BJ was in the county jail, I could not help but question what triggered him to rob someone. I needed him to be honest with me and take accountability for his wrongdoing. Regardless of what he said, there would be no excuse that would cause me to believe the malicious crime he was accused of would actually be justified. I was certain of one thing … I was not leaving Texas without the truth.

I am convinced there was not anything that could have prepared me for the meeting with this lawyer. I had a feeling of deception like never before but meeting with this man was the easy part. However, sitting there listening to the evidence that had been presented to him by detectives proved to be exhausting and traumatizing. While the words were disturbing, I knew I had to hear them in order to prepare myself for the inevitable future that waited in the shadows.

As much as I tried to change the narratives in my head, I needed to know the awful details of what BJ had done. I pictured myself in the shoes of the victim(s) versus presumptuously imagining what may have happened. As the lawyer continued to present evidence, along with dates and events, my heart continued to sink into grief and despair. Through this, I thought about his father and realized that his identity matched his father's identity. After spending an hour with the public defender, I told him that whatever he needed I was willing to help. We shook hands, and I was on my way to see my son for the first time in the county jail.

Driving to the jail, I prayed hard and asked God to transform my powerful role as a mother to a magnetic force drawing out the truth. I needed the truth from my son today; otherwise, I would never visit him again. I wanted him to comprehend entirely that under no circumstances would I accept the wrongdoing that he had done. I also wanted him to know without hesitation that I would love and support him unconditionally throughout his demise.

Walking into the jail, I was instructed sign in, present identification, and get into the line of others waiting. This atmosphere was so different and such a disappointment for me that I looked around in disbelief. There was a nice lady in front of me who was there to visit her son. She had arrived after a 10 hour bus ride from Oklahoma. The guards would not allow her to visit her son because she did not have the proper attire for the prison dress code. This lady was furious. It was entertainment for most, but it was a heartbreak for her. I proceeded in front of her for my fifteen minutes. I was shaking and my mind was racing; I was beyond nervous and scared. Not only had I not seen my son in nearly six months since the day he walked out, but now it would be in this jailhouse. After the humiliation of being searched fully clothed, I was allowed to see my son for behind a partitioned glass.

He walked in and I immediately noticed a huge transformation had taken place since we last saw one another. His once cold and dark eyes of the streets were now clear and back to their natural color. He looked like the old BJ, but with a remorseful tone. I spoke first. I point blank asked, "What did you do?" followed by "I do not want to hear a bold-faced lie, because I will turn around and walk away. Before you say anything, I want you to use the vitality of your presence and tell the truth, because that is what will get you through this." He looked up at me and said, "I did, but I did not act alone." Confident in conversation because it seemed like BJ was willing to tell me the truth but still unsettled at possible reasoning for this, I asked, "Why? If you needed money that bad, you could have called me. I have always given you what you needed." He looked at me with deep remorse and said, "Momma, it was not about the money. It was deeper than that."

Looking at him and answering the voice in my head, I blurted out, "Where did *this* come from? What were you thinking?" He answered, "Momma, I promise you that I did not hurt anyone. I had a play gun. I did not realize that it would turn out this way. It was the drugs and the peer pressure. This was not me." I said to him, "BJ, scaring someone is almost worse than harming or murdering them. It is an unforgiving torture that they think about every morning IF they can even sleep. How would you like it if someone robbed me with a play gun or any object for that matter? This is not good."

It was the fastest fifteen minutes I had ever experienced. Before I knew it, it was time for me to leave. I steadfastly told him, "I love you. I ask that you drop to your knees, pray, and ask God for forgiveness. We have a long road ahead of us. As your mother and not as a person who agrees with any wrongdoing that you have done, I will be by your side as long as I live. I want you to understand that what you did created a hole so big that only the mercy and grace of a judge will help you get out of it." Then I left the visitation room.

As I proceeded to walk out, the lady who I mentioned earlier was still sitting there. Clearly she did not know which way to turn. I could not imagine sitting on a bus for ten hours to see my son and I was not allowed. As broken as I was, I offered to take her to the nearest store to purchase something. She said "I have no money." The look in her eyes was the look that every mother has when you feel hopeless. I took my newly purchased St. John sweater off and said "please go see your son."

The drive back to Louisiana was much quicker than the drive to Texas. I had finally been able to look in my son's eyes, get the truth, and contemplate on everything during my drive home. There were long moments of crying, but it was senseless. All of the tears were wasted tears that were nothing more than liquid prayers. I knew my son did not truly understand the grave trouble that he had put himself in. If I could barely comprehend the harsh ramifications for his actions, I knew he certainly did not understand. One fact remained constant: this was not the BJ that I knew.

To be clear, this was not unconditional acceptance but rather unconditional love. As much as I loved him unconditionally, I could not accept this crime he had committed unconditionally. The only thing that lay ahead of him was a day of reckoning.

COLDEST DAY IN SEPTEMBER

"Expectations are resentments waiting to happen."
-Anne Lamott

Dressed in white prison attire, handcuffed and escorted to court by police officers, my son walked in labeled by a number and not by name with his arms and feet shackled. We waited a long nine months for this day; the day that a man was to decide my son's fate. I was optimistic. I was prepared to take him home with probation in lieu of a harsh jail sentence.

"Will the Defendant please rise?" These are words I have heard several times before, but only because I work in the legal system. I never imagined in a million years that I would be sitting in court as a mother of a defendant on trial in a criminal matter. I prepared for the best, not the worst. I had not concentrated on what the public defender told us to be prepared to hear from the Judge and prosecutor. A white man with an authoritative and powerful tone wearing a black robe spoke, *"You are hereby sentenced to forty consecutive years of hard labor in the Texas State Penitentiary."* I heard the words, but for a flashing moment, it was as if I were watching a movie or one of

those crime shows. Was this real? Forty years? In an instant, like the collapse of the buildings on 9/11, my world came crashing down.

Before sentencing, my son walked in with an expectation of hope and deliverance; after sentencing, he was transmogrified into a pillar to post statute. As soon as the sentencing was read, my son looked over at me perplexed and oblivious of what the judge had just spoken. His public defender put his head on the desk before pointing to the back of the courtroom for us to meet. For me, this was the moment of my greatest pain; also, denial. I sat there deafened, numb, and mortified. I had just witnessed my son sentenced to life in prison. Before being ushered out by officers, my son blew me a kiss and said, "I love you."

Barely audible, I asked, *"Grandma, did he just say forty years?"* She looked up at me with pain in her eyes and said, *"Yes, baby, he did."* I continued to sit paralyzed with doubt, but could hear myself uttering the words, *"This is so not happening."* I needed to tell someone. Someone validating that my feelings were normal is what I longed to hear. I needed to know that during this tragic time, at this very moment, it would be okay. Often times, I could talk myself out of a bad feeling or situation by thinking that something else could be so much worse or reminding myself that tomorrow is another day to get it right. Not this time. This time, I sat there in disbelief with self-pity feeling utterly broken. *"What just happened?"* I asked the public defender. He said, *"I don't know."* I thought to myself, "You don't know?? You don't know?!!?"

Walking out of that courtroom felt as if I was having a psychotic break. In fact, I am sure that I did. All I could see was darkness even though the sun was shining. I remember standing in front of a vending machine. As I blankly watched a woman push the button for the banana chips, I felt my heart fall, and the falling banana chips

25

reflected that. All I could hear over and over was, *"Forty years."* In the weeks prior, the lawyer had said PROBATION.

The lawyer walked over to me to console me saying, *"Mrs. Horne, I am so sorry, but if it would make you feel better, please file an appeal on grounds of ineffective assistance of counsel."* While the tears fell to no end, and my knees begin to buckle, I said, *"But you said......and I was only prepared for what you said. How can this Judge give my son forty years as a first-time offender?"* He responded with, *"This is all that I can suggest that you do."*

On my way out of court, there were so many parents who were entering and leaving the surrounding courtrooms. I could see the brokenness through their eyes and saw the pain in their body language. Mothers walking fast, biting their lips, heads held down, mumbling to themselves, and gritting their teeth ... all signs of insurmountable pain. In each courtroom that I walked passed, I heard more grasps than if I was in the foyer of a labor and delivery hospital. Those gasps were attestations of relief, grief or dismay and were all reflections of my feelings.

As I struggled to my car with an intoxicated walk, a piece of my sentimental value was just taken away. I did not have a damn thing to do with it nor there was anything that I could do about it. I felt like there was a runaway train coming straight for me.

This had to be the longest six-hour drive home. As my eighty-two-year old grandmother, the matriarch of our family and my biggest cheerleader, sat in the passenger seat trying to console me, her words were camouflaged with hearing the judge yell, *"Forty years."* As I drove, I continued to cry and silently had a brutal heart-wrenching conversation with GOD.

"GOD, you took my mom a year and a half ago, now my

oldest son. What is next? What is next? Why are you doing this to me? I work every single day. I am obedient to your almost every word and this is what I receive in return. Help me fix this Lord, please help me fix this. I cannot live like this. I know that my son made a mistake, but did he have to be your candidate? You have murderers and rapists. Why him? Why did you allow this Judge to give my son all this time?"

As we crossed the Louisiana state line, I pulled over and sat there crying for at least an hour. I cried for every mother who was feeling what I was feeling. I cried for every child who was parentless. I cried for every grandmother who was watching her granddaughter cry as my grandmother watched me. I let it all out until there was nothing left in me. Then I started the car and began driving again. While driving, I couldn't help but wonder what was going through my son's mind. The Judge's words, *"Forty years"*, kept screaming in my ears. I looked in my rearview mirror and saw the haunting image of my son turning his head toward me in slow motion saying, "NOOOOOOOO."

The minute I pulled into my grandmother's driveway, I knew that either one of two things were about to happen. I would go home and sleep my life away or I would put one foot in front of the other and come up with a plan. The latter happened, but it took time. I went home and wallowed in doubt and fear. I waited for the agonizing phone call I knew would come. Eventually, it did.

"Hey ma, I am so sorry. I don't know what to do. I can't do this. What can we do? I know that I was wrong, but I can't do forty years. I didn't kill anybody. I didn't hurt anybody and everybody in here can't believe the Judge gave me forty years. I don't deserve forty years. I'm eighteen years old. I will be fifty-seven years old when I get out of here. We have to file an

appeal or something. I can't do forty years in here. Momma, I should have listened."

As I listened to his pain, I was feeling my own pain. It did not help that I had just swallowed six Vicodin as an attempt to temporarily ease my pain with sleep. As he pleaded with a desperate cry for help, I was desperate for optimism. Each cry for help would be like a burglar vandalizing me and nobody was there to rescue me. With each of his cries, came two for me. Here I am working in the legal system, but there was not a damn thing that I could do.

As much as I wanted to say, *"This is what happens when you disobey your parents.",* I could not. Nothing could be gained by saying such words. I cried silently and responded, *"I am here for you. We must pray for change and, as disappointed as I am, my love for you will never waiver. We will get through this one day at a time. This is another obstacle that God has placed before us. We will overcome. Goodnight Son, I love you."*

As positive as I was trying to be, and trying to negate what I had just experienced, I could not forget the pain that I had just endured. For the past two years, my son had morally bankrupted me.

A MOTHER'S PAIN

Started off with birth pain, pain only a mother feels
Wishing she would have kept her legs closed like a window seal
She didn't and didn't abort me either
Determined to hold me like a telephone receiver
Nine months long - did it for nine months strong
Even with a big stomach and still as pretty as Nia Long
Then came emotional pain - raising me with two gigs
How hard she worked you would have thought she had two kids
Twenty-five years later she raised four of us
And even if she could - wouldn't let go of us
I'm locked behind steel - I can't even hold her
And every morning she wakes up, I'm steady getting older
That's pain you can't explain, pain hard to discuss
Pain you want to give up, harder than cold pizza crust
Pain make you want to cry
For better days we hopin'
Eyes red like she been swimming under water with both of them open
Make her want to take Tylenol PMs and sleep until they release me
Or until she take that trip upstate to come and see me
That pain that make you wanna call the Judge and question the sentence
Why give him forty years with no prior offenses
He was only seventeen - that's cruel and unusual
That's time you make a killer or a sex offender do
And she fell asleep every night feeling the same hurt
Seeing more pain than a hospital nurse
But working to minimize the anguish, get me away from wardens
Knowing I should be famous and performing in Madison Square Garden

But she move for me still and I admire her movement
That's the mother's pain and I am sorry I put you through
it.

THE DAYS AFTER RECKONING

"We are all different. Don't judge, understand instead."
-   Roy T. Bennett, The Light in the Heart

I woke up with bloodshot red eyes, my throat dry as a desert, and my mind still racing incessantly. All I could think of was the feelings my son must have been having at this very moment. I closed my eyes once again and pinched myself as what I had just gone through could not have been real. I turned to the nightstand and stared at the prescription bottle of Vicodin. I wanted to take the pills to forget that any of this was happening, but I knew it was far more necessary to become proactive not numb.

The first thing I did was call my doctor, who often doubled as my psychologist, for an appointment. I needed someone to talk to who did not quite know what was going on, but who could empathize with what I had to tell him. I needed to feel the enormity of my pain so that I could illustrate what I was feeling. I had an appointment in three days. Until my appointment, I wallowed in guilt, pain, regret, disappointment, and remorse. I swallowed Vicodin and Ambien to get to sleep. At times, I would get lost in nostalgia as I listened to songs that Blake would sing or watched television programs that we would watch together.

I was inundated with phone calls, e-mails, and knocks at my door. For the most part, it was people who had heard of the sentencing and just wanted to intrude. I didn't want sympathy. I could not handle hearing the usual *"Oh God, not Blake."* or *"How could this happen to you?"* I ignored anyone's attempts to contact me. I knew that my attitude was scathing. There were only two things that could help me ... God and time.

Despite numerous failed attempts to speak with the public defender, I persisted, because I needed to know if there was anything I could do to have this conviction overturned. As usual, I only received his voice mail message. One day, I decided on a final attempt to e-mail him.

Dear Mr. X,

I need to fix this. This has literally made me numb with knowing that BJ has gotten forty years. My son said he cannot do forty years, which literally has me thinking he will commit suicide. I have been up for three nights sitting here and wondering how the judge could give my son forty years. I will be dead in forty years. How could you go from preparing me for probation to this judge firmly saying forty years? We should have tried this case instead of letting the judge decide his fate. This judge seemed to have his mind made up. I need to prepare a writ of habeas corpus myself and a notice of appeal, but I do not know what grounds I have to do this. Please help? I need a way to turn.

I waited patiently for him to respond and he did. His response was very cold and unbothered.

Mrs. Horne,

There was the potential that if this case was tried, he could have gotten life. This judge gave a juvenile with multiple aggravated robberies probation a short time ago, so I was correct in thinking that he would fairly consider probation for a person as young as your son. As far as leading you to believe that he would get probation, I told you what I thought and I worked hard to achieve that goal.

I will file an appeal Monday and BJ will get a new attorney who will work with you to place the blame on me. If successful, BJ could face those same charges again. Once again, he may be successful in placing the blame for his situation on someone else. All I can say is I did the best that I could. I don't believe that the sentence was fair, but I am confident that a jury would have been worse.

I think it would be better if you did not contact me again because I understand that your goal would be to find a way to blame me. I hope that you understand that I have grief of my own and I wish and prayed and worked for BJ to escape a prison sentence. But the result was dictated by facts.

After reading this, I felt very indifferent. I kept thinking about how he thought it was not fair, but it could have been worse. I was confused and did not know exactly how to take this all in. Again, I was faced with the ugly truth. He thought that because another child with multiple aggravated robberies was given probation, that my son would be given the same? There were so many questions I wanted to ask. "Was this child the same race as my son?" "Did his parents donate money to the judge's political campaign?" "Was this a political favor?" "Was this decision made before Obama got into office or after?" "Did this kid have a private lawyer or a public defender?" Instead, I respected his request and never contacted him again.

I desperately needed my mom's presence. I needed her to come down from Heaven and remind me that this too shall pass. I wanted her to reassure me that no matter what happened to me now, God would guide me every step of the way. Even though deep down I knew all of the wise words she would give me, I could not muster the strength to find them. I was not yet in a place to pull myself up from the abyss of the despair I was feeling. I was incredibly vulnerable and certainly not ready to let my inflated ego be nullified by society. There was no way to know how I would be treated, but I was as timid as a baby and like a baby, I needed to be desensitized.

I continued to self-medicate. I did not bathe for days. Everything I ate only found its way out of my system. I lay in bed struggling to remember what inner peace felt like. With every attempt to rise up from the hollows of my grief came the realization of life – my son had just received forty years in prison with no chance of parole for twenty years. I discovered what rock bottom felt like and I knew the only way to go up from here was to recognize there was a way to do so. God would have to save me because trying to handle this on my own seemed unbearable. There was no way I could get through this without God's grace, strength, and loving embrace.

FEW DAYS LATER

As I continued to process all that had happened, this was the first day that I humbly embraced my true feelings. I had come to terms with my feelings. I exposed my truth to my doctor exposing everything that I was going through. The minute I walked into his office, he greeted me with a kind and comforting smile as if he already knew I would be confessing my secret to him.

> Me: Doctor, I'm depressed and I need help. I feel delusional. I feel like I cannot go on anymore and, as cliché as this may sound to you, I feel hopeless and helpless. You are my confessional booth today as you were when my mom passed away.

After explaining every detail of the events leading up to the trial and the weeks following the trial, we talked for some time. One of the most noteworthy parts of our conversation went like this:

> Dr.: Mrs. Horne, your blood pressure is really low and your weight has dropped significantly. I know that you have other children. How are they doing?

> Me: They are great.

> Dr.: Are you sure? How are you aware if all you do is self-medicate and sleep?

> Me: Fair enough – I stand to be corrected. I do not know, but I know that my husband is making sure that they are eating and going to school. He is fully aware that I am going through immense difficulty at this time."

> Dr.: Mrs. Horne, I know that you are

going through a very difficult time
and it may seem your darkest days
will never end, but if you do not get
a grip on this, you will be dead in a
matter of weeks.

Leaving the doctor's office, I knew I was experiencing an enormous shift in my life. To hear the doctor say to me, *"If you do not get a grip on this, you will be DEAD in a matter of weeks,"* was absolutely life changing. Talking to myself, answering myself at the same time, and feeling like I was the only person in the world experiencing this left me feeling exhausted constantly. My mind always brought me back to my heart. Though I tried to cease thinking about what was happening around me, I never stopped thinking about how my son must have been feeling.

The beginning of my son's unforgiving jail sentence felt like an ending to me. With such cruelty, the words "why are we here and how did we get here" endlessly repeated in my mind. Many times, I felt like a runaway train had come straight for me; though, at other times, I felt like God was saving me from yet another tragedy only He knew could exist.

In the coming days, my inner strength gradually returned as I slowly began freeing myself from the pain and illusion of endlessness. Nevertheless, I harbored fear of not knowing what would happen in the years to come. I also felt angry with myself for not doing more and remained confused as to why this had happened at all. I had to promise myself that I would continue to push forward while waiting on an appeal. The reality was that I had a business to operate, a job to perform, and people to please not to mention the fact that I had four children that counted on me, which included BJ. There was no other option than to continue to be their guiding light regardless of my feelings. They did not choose me; I could not abandon them.

NEW NORMAL

"I didn't want normal until I didn't have it anymore."
-Maggie Stiefvater, Lament

Crying and not knowing what to expect, I sat on an airplane in complete and utter disbelief. My entire world had changed before my very own eyes. I was flying to a place I never thought I would find myself. February 11, 2010 ... my first visit to a state penitentiary.

The moment I stepped off the plane onto the jetway, the butterflies started to swarm in my stomach. I felt like I was suspended in motion. After retrieving my bags and a rental car, I was off into a world that I never dreamed of visiting. As I set out on the long drive, the miles turned into an abyss of nothing more than land and cattle. Real people, houses, or stores were nonexistent. The external forces were finally settling in. This was the realist depiction of a four-year journey that any parent could ever receive.

I had several bouts of anxiety, several bouts of crying spells, and all I was left with was a vicious view of the judge who convicted my son to forty years in prison. *"Will the Defendant please rise,"* echoed in and out of my ear like a never-ending sonic boom. The drive seemed to reduce the quality of my life into mental torture. With no signal for my cell phone, I had no one to talk to, so I started talking to myself. *"Why in the hell would they put a prison in an inaccessible area?" "I know this had to be agony for the inmates riding on a bus for hours chained from Houston to Lamesa."*

I finally approached a sign stating, "The Smith Unit." I had arrived and would finally be reunited with my son, even if only for a brief period of time. I was welcomed by a nice officer who kindly stated, *"Name of the inmate you are seeing and TDCJ number. Ma'am, please pop your hood and trunk please."* Despite everything that I had already gone through, I now found myself subjected to a search from a female guard before I could see my son. *"Is this the norm?"* I asked. She answered with a simple nod implying that it was. I observed the barb wired fence and the officers sitting in the tower with their guns cocked and ready to fire. All I could think about was how no one would escape from this place. If they tried, the road only led to death.

Waiting impatiently and watching other parents go through their extensive search, I was astonished that there were more mothers than fathers. "Where are all the patriarchies of the family?", I thought. Why are there more Mexicans and African Americans than any other race? As I sat there and observed the indescribable atmosphere, I quickly noted that we all had something in common. We were all there to visit someone in prison that we loved beyond explanation.

Suddenly a loud screeching noise sounded off and the gates opened. Everyone lined up like this was procedure. Being my first time, I pursued behind the last person as if this was procedural. As I entered the gates of hell, the screeching noise sounded off yet again behind me to let me know that I was now in a place of brokenness and I had to accept the next four hours on correctional facility terms.

With each door's opening and closing, the more I appreciated the outside world and all its shortcomings. I appreciated my viable options and the imperfect world I represent. But today, it was not about me … it was about my son.

The last door finally closed, and I remained patient in a room with other parents. What I found to be more astounding than anything is how calm these parents were and how accustomed they were to this environment. Many of them knew each other. They joked and laughed about their truths which were very uncomfortable to me. Maybe someday this would be universal language, but today this prison jargon seemed barbarous. I learned there was an African-American woman who would see her son for an hour and then would leave to drive another three hours to see another son who was at another penitentiary. My heart stopped for a quick second after learning that.

The attending guard began to call several names and my name was one of them. He escorted me into a cafeteria with vending machines and told me that I could purchase whatever I wanted; however, the duty guard would need to remove the tops off drinks and remove snacks out of the wrapper. *Why?"* I asked. He responded, *"Precautionary measures."* There were several round tables like picnic tables where inmates and their families sat. I nervously stood my ground waiting for my son to enter. I didn't know what to expect. I did not know if my son had been altered in any way. All I knew was I wanted to see my oldest son walk in as the person I left sitting in that cold and horrified courtroom in September.

BJ walked in with that beautiful smile showing his pearly white teeth just as I had always remembered. He looked the same, but his demeanor was noticeably different. He looked like a cub coming out of his cage for the first time to meet his maker. I was greeted with a great big hug until the officer said, *Enough."* *"What do you mean enough?"* I asked firmly. BJ said in a matter of fact tone, *"Momma, these people are prejudice and they do not care, so we must abide or they will strip my right of visitation."*

I sat there knowing something was different about my

son. This was a new normal for both of us. As we talked, he looked around nervously. *"Why are you looking around and beside you?"* I asked. He responded, *"Mom, this is prison and no one can be trusted."* I had so many questions. How do you wash clothes? What do you eat? How is it in this place? With each question, there were answers that I did not want to hear. Of course, I did not expect him to be eating gumbo, but I did not expect him to say bologna sandwiches either.

I sat there enjoying my son's conversation, but I could not help but look around and see the collateral damage of a bunch of broken families, including my own. There were mothers and fathers visiting their kids, kids visiting their parents, and babies being awakened by the noise of prisoners. I was born into a new state of conscious. I was often distracted by the vision of my surroundings. My identity was stripped by the four walls of this prison lifestyle and a moment of extreme helplessness.

The four-hour visit seemed more like five minutes. When it was time to depart, I hugged my son as if I was leaving him on the first day of school. This time it was different. It would be awhile before I would see him, again. I walked out of that prison and I broke down as if this was the last time I would see him again. I left feeling cold, indifferent, and out of touch. This would be the new normal for me. I suddenly realized that this was not a journey of my own anymore; this was everything short of miraculous.

A DIFFERENT WORLD by BJ

When the gates close and the doors lock
Life gets hotter than supper and you are just a number
Owned by the state, three hots in a cot
And this world is mad dirty like old kitchen mops
Extremely polarized - divided by gang affiliation
Where inmates get high off of mental illness medication
A lot of men can take it, don't know what to do
I've seen a man hang himself, just to die a little soon
A world where blacks are the majority and whites the
minority
Correctional officers like to abuse the authority
Brutal killings with knives - but not the ones in your
kitchen
I'm talking about the ones made from pieces of iron
fences
See your mom can be mourning at any given morning
After a "I'm sorry for your loss" phone call from the
Warden
Where weak-minded men get raped and extorted
So if you are not strong, you can end up like Tracy
Morgan
A world where inmates do laundry in their toilet
Lay wool blankets on the floor and pretend that it's
carpet
It's a mind thing - alteration of the mental
Dream to erase the written past wishing life was a pencil
Loyalty don't exist anymore - the trust is gone
Like a street off a freeway you easily get turned on
Your life is out of shape living in the worst form
So many blacks in this can like cream corn
Needing someone to lean on, visits are like Christmas

Letters telling you how they miss us and will never
forget us
That they truly forgive us for leaving them like that
No matter what – they are waiting for us to come back
In this world these words are like a kiss
From my grandmother who died in December 2006
Who gave me that healthy love although she was sick
These are the small things that matter in the world I'm
livin'

GENETICS V. ENVIRONMENT

"The laws of genetics apply even if you refuse to learn
them."
-Allison Plowden

I never knew the real effects of *Generational Curse* and
Iniquities until I was doing research on influence. In
church, I would hear these words often but never knew the
real meaning. I certainly never thought I would experience
such words in my own life. While I'm more spiritual, I do
hold a belief in the power of God. I have always believed
He allows things to happen in this universe when it is
meant to be, not when I demand it. When my life became
consumed with chaos, the person I ran to for refuge was
God. I needed guidance and, more importantly, I needed
answers because everything seemed so incomprehensible.
Questions came like a tidal wave to my mind. Had I not
been a good mother? Where had I gone wrong? What
should I have done differently? It was during this time of
self-doubt and self-judgment that I began to learn about the
power of generational curses and iniquities.

I pondered why I was going through so much turmoil
with my eldest son. All of my children were so creative and
studious. I was raising them with the same teachings and
within the same environment. My then-husband and I were
model parents. We never smoked or drank alcohol. Our
work ethic was impeccable. We went to church
occasionally to get spiritually fed. We were believers and

prayed individually, as a family, with our children, and for our children.

I was plagued by the incessant need to understand how so much havoc had entered our lives by one child ... a child whose environment was no different than our other children. My thoughts spun around in a vicious cycle day after day longing for answers to the same questions. What was he thinking? Why had he made this choice? What did we do wrong to deserve this terrible pain? Why was my love unwavering despite the disorder and confusion brought on by this child? We have three other children to focus our attention upon; yet, we still focused on our now-troubled son. I knew what God promised me through prayer, so I kept praying. When would I have the answers I so desperately sought?

Just when I thought I could not take another day of these burning questions encompassing my every thought, God answered in the most peculiar way. I mindlessly grabbed the remote control and turned on my television. T.D. Jakes' sermon, *Breaking the Cycle*, was on the channel. I listened and immediately became enthralled by his words. His sermon confirmed what I had been feeling all this time. It was as though he was speaking only to me. In five words, he answered my questions: My son was his father. I heard T.D. Jakes state the following:

> *"God created Adam in his likeness and his image. A blessed God creates a blessed son. Everything in life produces after its own kind. Anytime a father is cursed, the son is cursed. There is no way a cursed father could produce a blessed son. The sin curse passes from generation to generation."*
> *"Sometime or other before your life is over, you have got to fight your daddy's devil."*
> *"Sooner or later, the same thing that came*

*against your dad, that same thing will come
against you."*

I ran straight to the Bible. I read scripture after scripture flipping the pages anxiously reading with intensity. Two scriptures in particular stood out:

> Exodus 34:7: "Keeping Mercy for thousands, forgiving iniquity and transgression and sin, and that will by no means clear the guilty; punishing the iniquities of their fathers upon their children, and upon the children's children, until the third and fourth generation."

> Lamentations 5:7: "Our fathers have sinned, and are not; and we have borne their iniquities."

Those scriptures answered so many of my questions as to why my oldest son was different from my other sons. While he was part of the same household, he had a different father and this went beyond learned behavior or environment. This was a deep-rooted issue. This was genetic. As many times as I had condemned myself, I was finally given absolution from my own doubt. Things had suddenly become so transparent to me. I now wondered who was to blame for all of this. Was it his father's fault or his grandfather's fault? How far back did this go? My eldest son had embraced the same life of his father by running away and turning to drugs and chaotic adventures that left his life in utter turmoil.

In the forty years of my existence, I had never read the bible nor researched the scriptures as much as I did that day. I had finally regained my willpower and emotional strength to move forward. I saw my son's life through the eyes of the beholder. It made me sick and morally bankrupt to realize that I was an active participant in my son's jail sentence.

Because of my imperfections and lack of common sense, I allowed myself to become involved with a person who never confronted the demons that he was faced with; that generational curse was not yet broken and those chains were linked to me through a number of differences. Ultimately, I was influenced to let this broken and imbalanced person plant a seed in soil that was so wet and weak that another growing plant would be just as imbalanced. I wondered if my son even had the chance to be dominant. Before my research, I would have emphatically said "yes" because of the positive traits that we both (somewhat) possessed; however, there were still generational defects that were coming against my son. Ultimately, it was only by his choice that he would have been saved from his father's generational curse.

I have thought extensively about the equities that I have produced out of all of this and have come to the conclusion that my other children had become the equities. They are no better than my eldest; however, they did not possess a trait of having either parent born into a curse of criminal behavior.

My grandfather did mad time behind bars
His son raised by prison guards due to a drug
charge
His son indicted on five cases had a stick up
crew
DA dismissed three on the strength he plead
guilty to two
Two years later little brother is locked up
Robbery went sour and somebody got shot
He signed for fifteen years, my time didn't alarm
him

Co-Defendant got less time "cus" he turned
state evidence on them
Four Generations - Four Incarcerations
What goes around, comes around, medical neck
braces
Now we are only seeing freedom in high hope
dreams
Half the family can touch cans but not soda
machines
Say it's a generational curse, affiliated by birth
Poisonous bloodstream born with toxic genes
Are we destined to be criminals, is that really the
fate?
Are our lives supposed to have more holes than
milk crates?
Take us away from our mothers and makes their
hearts shatter
Now they're having therapeutic meetings crying
to church pastors
History repeats itself, the past conceives the
present
This is the reason blacks see more cells than text
messages
Main reason prisons look like black
neighborhoods
And so many men being stored like can goods
Generational curse, a curse we had to accept
One after another like staircase steps

Read those words again. Thought provoking, right? When you really think about generational traits and the strength of one's genes, self-destructive behavior, as with any other behavior, becomes part of the family's bloodline. Alcoholics breed alcoholics, racism breeds racism, wealth breeds wealth, and so on. We must also face the realization that criminals breed criminals. Interestingly, most of these traits are transformative when a child is born into the family, not when one is adopted. Additionally, you realize that environmentally-learned behavior also comes into effect.

We all deal with a family legacy of addictions or negativity of some kind. Uncomfortably, we must confront what likely goes back many generations. Now that I am aware, I ask myself questions such as, "What am I passing down to my children whether through generations or environment?" "Will I allow the addictions of my family to imprison me or will I take full responsibility and make better choices while releasing the bondage over my life?"

To every young person, I impress upon them to look with grave intent at a person's background before committing one's body, soul, and heart to them. Dysfunctional and behavioral patterns are often passed down from parents to children and, sadly, become models in one's environment. During my youth, I was a rebellious and selfish teenager who made many self-imposed decisions never once thinking about how those decisions would affect my future. I admit that the choices I made to give my life to a man born into criminality and generational disadvantages ultimately impacted my son's life. As a result, he is serving a forty-year sentence, and now, I harbor an immense amount of guilt, regret, and heartbreak.

THE POWER

"No matter what happens or how bad it seems today, life
does go on, and it will be better tomorrow."
-Maya Angelou

DEAR SON

BJ:

Like most teenagers my age, I wanted to be "accepted" and "validated" from a certain group of peers. I did not know being an on-the-scene person would bring so many unfortunate events. Being so cost you your life, and I am so sorry for that. My mom always told me that wanting to grow up fast would cost more than you could ever bargain for. She could not have been more right.

Your dad was handsome, street smart, and part of the popular group. That was so appealing to me at the time because I wanted to be noticed. I wanted to be popular. I wanted so badly to fit in with the in-crowd. Son, I never did anything like engage in drugs or go to jail, but I did skip school. I had sex at a very young age. I disrespected my parents, and I made many mistakes. The biggest mistake I made was getting pregnant at the age of sixteen with someone I thought I loved.

I realize now that I was too young to know anything about being in love. I thought material possessions and your father being possessive or even beating me were all attestations of his love for me. With fierce vengeance, your father would punch me leaving black eyes and kick me in the stomach; yet, I continued to comply. I was so broken, I never fought back. He was my heroin and I was addicted to him. No matter how many people, including his own mother, told me that he was no good for me, he was still my drug of choice.

It was not until I was in the hospital giving birth to you that I learned the true meaning of love. With my mom and grandmother by my side, I was surrounded by love and felt real love. Here I was at seventeen, an uneducated teenage mother with an uneducated teenage boyfriend having a child. Unlike my parents who were raised with both parents, lived in a suburban home, graduated high school, went to college, and tried to praise me every chance that they could, I gave them little to celebrate.

The first time I held you in my arms, I knew I needed to do better. Even so, your father walked right back into my life and began manipulating me, again. He promised me that he would do better for me … for us. Just like every time before, my vulnerability set in, and I believed him. I did not want to rob you of your birthright. I wanted the American dream. I wanted a beautiful family with you and my handsome boyfriend. That would include his abuse, drug dealing, and cheating, but I didn't want to think about those things. I was so weak before I had you and I thought that you would somehow make me whole. I did not know I was actually breaking you.

After six months of constant lies and abuse, I refused to run the gauntlet again. I remember this moment as if it were yesterday. I left the welfare office to get on the public bus. I sat down and looked into your beautiful brown eyes, and started sobbing. Through my tears I said, "I will make you proud of me. I got this. We have got this. God's got this." You looked up at me and giggled. To me, that meant that you were up for the challenge with me. It was you and me, kid, against the world. I needed to grow up and be better for you. I knew it wouldn't be easy, but I was ready to accept the challenges and happy to move forward no matter what came our way.

Putting you in daycare, I dropped out of school to work my ass off at any odd job I could find until I was able to go back to school and provide a better life for us. When my friends were going out, I was coming home from working these jobs to make sure you had everything that you needed. It gave me great pleasure to know I was taking care of you.

Like present day, I had a mission to complete and you to save. I also had something to prove to all the naysayers, including my own family who incessantly chanted "you will never amount to anything." Statistics would have proven them right had we not fought against them.

Son, you were my life. Before I would go to sleep at night, I would ask you, "Am I doing a good job as your mother?" I was so afraid of so many uncertainties. Many nights, I would go in the bathroom and just cry. Then I would come out, look at you, and smile so you always felt reassured that everything was going to be alright. Each day I was stronger. I mastered my strengths and managed my weaknesses. Life was seemingly getting better and our dreams were slowly coming to pass.

Then there were all the milestones. I do not know if you remember this because you were only three, but you and I danced at my wedding to Regina Belle's "If I Could." I would sing that song to you every morning while we drove to your school. Remember when you were eight and made that bomb-ass touchdown? No, wait, remember when you were ten and Cousin Donna talked us into putting you in dance school? Here you were taking dance classes in a predominately white dancing school and loving it. On top of that, the following year you started taking ballet classes. You were the only black boy until your brother joined you.

What was more impressive is that you always seemed to steal the show. I remember sitting in rehearsals and an older woman saying, "I come here just to see this little boy dance." Then there was the Nutcracker with the infamous ballet instructor, Ballet Hysell. Do not forget the video when you played Lil Wayne in his first video or the movies, commercials and off-Broadway productions in New York. We went from me being seventeen on welfare to twenty-five buying our first home to owning a business at twenty-eight. All of this was because of you first and then your brothers to follow. I wanted so desperately to give you and your siblings the world. I will hold these milestones in my heart forever.

BJ, we grew together and you were my best friend. You were my precious first born and from the depths of my being, I would make sure you were protected from anything that left you troubled. We had finally outgrown the statistic that people placed upon us and were afforded opportunities that the below-average Negro family would never outlive. We were rebels and born for greatness!

At twenty-five, you are still my baby, and I promise to be there for you until the day I die. I go to sleep with you on my mind and in my heart and I wake up the same. My prayer every single day is that I am alive to see you walk out of that inhumane cage that you are trapped in. I gave birth to you with a broken heart, and I would hate to die with a broken heart as a result of not being able to see you as a free man. If I could go back and change anything that I have ever done, I would have said no more often. I would have fought for you to stop you from walking out that door on your way to Texas to live with your father. Please forgive me for not doing so.

While you are in there, I want you to honor God within you. While there are many dimmed lights in there, brighten yours as bright as you can so others will follow in your pursuit. I believe in you and I know that the inside of that prison needs you. I know your heart is as big as gold. For others, you may be out of sight and out of mind, but for me, I will be right there with you until the day I close my eyes for the last time. I love you so much and, together, we shall always rise. I am who I am today because of you. Thank you, my beloved son.

Mom

DEAR MOMMA

I never asked to be a part of this world, but I was technically forced to. I was forced to make decisions that someone my age should never have been imposed to make. I was put in a position that I was not ready for. It is hard to ignore a child that is screaming for help unless you are content with what is making him scream silently to the top of his lungs. I do not believe that you were content, but when I first told you of the physical and mental abuse, I never asked you why you did not take action. I just asked you to keep me away from your cold-hearted husband. I always told you that I did not feel comfortable around him, but I know that you did.

What I do not understand is how your good parenting skills outweighed your unfortunate parenting skills and the less fortunate still wound up being the forefront and took total control of my life. To this day, I still do not understand how the present is the total opposite of where I am actually supposed to be in life. To be honest with you mom, as I sit here, and write this letter and think about things, I clearly understand that disloyalty became a negative force, which corrupted our lives. It corrupted the way we thought and the way we moved. We let two disloyal men, my father and your ex-husband, come between us like meat between two slices of bread.

Why?

Especially knowing that we were being pulled apart by such a negative force, and then, you divorced him once I got forty years. "Life is a bitch." (Excuse my language). Do you think things would have been different for me if you would have divorced him when you knew and understood how much he was the sinister of our immediate circle? I believe so. Is that disloyal? Is it disloyal that I talked back to you or kept running away or every time I got suspended from school you had to risk losing your job so that you could bring me back to school and have a parent/teacher conference? Is it? Is it disloyal that I did not attend my grandmother's funeral, and I was only around the corner from the funeral home? Is it disloyal that I left my younger brothers to come to the penitentiary knowing how much they looked up to me?

To answer all of those question ... yes, very disloyal. We both let each other down. We both made mistakes. By us being emotional people who are often misunderstood, we allowed our emotions to take over our mental.

Before you misinterpret me, please understand that it is all about intention. Did you intend to do what you did by staying in that marriage? I do not think so. You are my queen, my mother, my best friend, and the most reliable person that I know. The loyalty that you have shown me since I have been locked up is the best thing that has happened to me and the best gift that I have received in my twenty-five years of living. The respect that I have for you is about as long as St. Charles Avenue. I admire your strong womanhood; I have never met a woman with so much strength. Everyone makes mistakes in life, but it is a must we learn from them and let experience be the best teacher. I love you.

When I come home, we got to get back to how we used

to be. We were like brother and sister. Honestly, it is hard for me in here, but karma is a bitch. Everything that I put you through is being transferred back to me and I deserve it, but I was put under some raw circumstances. Maybe, I knew the right thing to do, but without wisdom, I became something I never wanted to be. Now, I am in a place where loyalty does not exist, and love is like finding Wesley Snipes in a tanning salon.

As I am writing this letter, I am wishing I was next to you. Wishing I could squeeze your feet like you used to ask me to do after a long day at work but I cannot. The love that you show, I have never had anyone, but you show that so unconditionally. You are amazing! Like I said, it is all about intention. I believe without a doubt in my mind that your intentions were truly sincere. For that, sometimes I wish you would not have ever met my father, and you never would have birthed me. I would rather not exist before being a disloyal son. I apologize for not understanding the importance of loyalty much sooner.

You are my heart and soul; you only did what you felt was right, and that is understood. Just know that it is hard in here, but I am going to keep fighting gravity, because I truly believe loyalty will prevail.

I love you!

BJ

A LESSON LEARNED

It's hard not to feel discouraged from all the cynic coverage
When you have something powerful that can better the
masses
That can help your life become sweeter than Easter baskets
The madness that you go through - past moves you misuse
Not knowing them woes - make your life harder than tap
shoes
Bad news that you will encounter with the years that come
People dislike you for what you have done
Treat you smaller than bread crumbs
As if it will make them sick to taste the flavor of your
person
It's hurting - the judgmental essentials rather disturbing
How can I transfer my true thoughts to you
So you can understand as a man what I am able to do
Please realize that children transform to grown-ups
Become wiser and more reluctant to engage in the wrong
stuff
Honestly why would I bluff to convince you or pretend to
Or waste my time writing rhymes unless I intend to
Work hard to change society, speak at detention centers
To kids who need guidance - whose role models are crack
dealers
To little girls who have working single mothers
That skip school to be with dudes who really don't love
them
I'll advise them that they should change and how much I
want to help them
That I will feel more responsible if I didn't take time to tell
them
Prisons are not for humans, they are the worst place ever
It's meant to make you suffer and freedom is so much
better
If you love your mom - you would not do this bad stuff

Because she loves you till death and it kills her when you
are locked up
It makes her cry when the Judge says "40 years"
She can't even drive 'cause her vision is blurry from all the
tears
Now she feels weird because she can't help you
'Cause for seventeen years straight, she was trying to tell
you
Do right son - life is too damn short
You don't want to be like your dad - that is not too damn
smart
Fast living - not worth going to prison for decades
And between then and now - your parents pass away
Your siblings get older and start making kids
You don't get one letter from people you thought were your
friends
You finally come to a conclusion that this does not make
sense
Because now you are not the same person that you were
back then

A PARENT'S CONVICTION

"Turn your wounds into wisdom." - Oprah Winfrey

WOW! Immediately after reading the letter from my son, my first reaction was to go into attack mode. To say I was angry was a grave understatement. My second reaction was to cry until I could not cry anymore. My gut instinct was to write a letter back exclaiming, "After all I have sacrificed and done for you, and continue to sacrifice for you, you have the nerve to send such a letter to me?" I knew better because I could foresee his response being, "If you would have divorced this man, I would not be where I am today." Nothing else that he wrote mattered. Did I inadvertently miss something that I should have been more aware of?

His letter was such a hard pill to swallow, because I had reached my full capacity to digest such words. After the hell I had been put through, the last thing I wanted to learn was that my son was actually blaming me for his demise. I had to marinate on this very notion for quite some time and it was not long before an epiphany came to me. I realized he was not blaming me, but rather, simply expressing his feelings. Who was I to invalidate what he felt?

As I contemplated the means of discipline that my ex-husband used, it became all too clear that they matched that of my mother which I hated. It was obvious he would feel the same way. Unlike BJ, I made it through my youth without the choices of my sometimes-imperfect behavior catching up to me. I recognize now that the recipe of my success was a direct result of my mother being hard on me. Even when I thought she was failing me, she was actually saving me.

My son knew right from wrong. My son knew that if he didn't clean his room that he would be punished and would not be allowed to play outside. He knew that if he disrespected authority at school, it would warrant a parent-teacher conference. He knew that committing a crime could be met with serious consequences.

While I take accountability, I will not take personal accountability for his choices. My accountability comes as a parent who was not always consistent, which I see now was the biggest mistake I made as BJ's mother. I was never consistent when saying "no." I often gave in and allowed him to break small rules such as breaking curfew or something as small as feeling sorry for him on a two-week punishment and letting him off a week early. When this occurred, he was unknowingly conditioned to not trust me to follow through with keeping my word. Children understand your expectations, but if you never enforce your words with actions, they easily learn they can get away with just about anything. How can you place standards and expectations on a child when you are not consistent?

As he mentioned in his letter, it is all about intention. Intention is something I never thought about until it was mentioned in my son's letter. I dug deep and did some serious soul searching, and I was able to see something in myself that I never saw before. In every aspect of my life, I always carried the best intentions even if it hurt me or other people. It hurt me to say 'no" to anyone. I would feel bad telling anyone no or that I could not go somewhere they asked me to go. As a result, I would always say "yes" even if I had no intention of going. If I did go, it was harbored with resentment, because the truth was I did not want to go.

I felt obligated to say "yes" to avoid disappointment for the other person.

In the moment of my greatest pain, I was still trying to make sense of what he was feeling when he said, "We let each other down." I cried and cried until my eyes were swollen and there were no more tears to shed. Suddenly, and without warning, like a lightning bolt from God, the answer came to me. As much as my view of things may have differed from his, it did not matter. His letter defined his truth ... his reality ... and it was liberating him. I never knew that opening up past wounds were so painful; I allowed myself to feel until I got exactly what he was feeling and that is when my feelings became therapeutic.

My intentions as a parent were to never allow anyone to hurt my son. My intent was to make my son follow the rules to become a better adult. I had to put the bulletproof armor on for him because his armor was full of people who were weak. I knew that if any enemy was after him, those weak people would soon turn their backs on him. I thought this was the healthiest part of my personality, but it was not. I was faced with this admission by my son who is sitting in a prison cell with nothing but time to reflect on what could have been different.

One particular question comes to mind often ... could life have been different? This is not a question I can answer nor will I ever know the answer. What I know is that I worked really hard to exceed expectations that I set for myself and my children. I was so busy trying to make things happen for all of us that I simply forgot to pay closer attention to what was going on in his reality. Despite the fact that I thought I was paying attention to every aspect of our lives, it is clear that there were things I overlooked or did not even see at all.

As parents, when there is a "different" child in the household, we will bend the rules and overcompensate for what we think the child is lacking. We tend to treat the child who no longer lives with both parents as the different child. We overcompensate which can be very daunting, and we do it because we feel guilty. When we find ourselves being a single parent, we have allusions circling in our minds that tend to cause us to parent in guilt. The fact is that parenting in guilt will have you making the wrong decisions each and every time. There is no room for guilt.

To me, my son was my world. To him, he was the different child in the house. He was the stepchild – the child whose last name was different. He should have had the same chances to have greater opportunities. Every disciplinary action was tainted, because the man that raised him as his own was not actually his paternal father. For BJ, this experience was a painful one. For me, learning my son felt this way is just another cross that I must bear for not knowing if things would have been different had I chosen differently.

All of these mishaps make my conviction as a parent personal. Despite my best efforts, I now realize that I failed on several levels. My first failure began at age sixteen when I decided not to be responsible with my body. I did not have a solid contingency plan. I failed by not paying attention to the background of my son's father. I failed at being a normal teenager. Most important, I failed in making decisions that would have resulted in better choices for me. As a result of those poor decisions, a child gave birth to a child out of wedlock. Emotionally, I was fragile. I did the best I could using the experiences from the women before me, but that was not good enough. I was as a woman fighting for a place in a boy's heart only to fail at being who I should have been at sixteen years old … a child, not a woman.

Like so many young people, my identity was misplaced. I was operating on autopilot going through all sorts of emotions, yet my mind was stuck at a place of immaturity. To go deeper on this, every child's dream is for their parents to be together forever. When this does not happen, it is a disservice to them and it affects their entire being. By not choosing a better father for my son, another generation of dysfunction was created. At sixteen, I was not ready for a relationship much less a child. The reality is that when you become involved in a relationship you are not ready for and a child is produced, that child becomes the target of every dart thrown in the parents' direction. My decisions directly correlate with the fact that my son is taking a dart for the next thirty years.

As much as I wanted everything to fall in place, it did not. As much as I thought everything was normal, it was not. One of the greatest blessings in our lives is to bear children, but we must remind ourselves that they are not responsible for the families they are born into. That responsibility lies within us. We must do the due diligence to ensure our relationships are in the best interest of any children we may conceive. Otherwise, we may actually be responsible for setting up our children up for failure and disappointment.

I AM MY SON'S KEEPER

"Being ignored by someone who
means the world to you is the worst feeling." –Unknown

What I know for certain is that we are all part of our children's pain and suffering. Therefore, what exactly is pain? The definition of pain is physical suffering or discomfort caused by illness or injury. Examples of pain and suffering are aches, temporary and permanent limitations on activity, potential shortening of life, and depression or scarring.

The pain and suffering of a parent is usually silent much like their cries even though their hearts tend to make a lot of necessary noise. Instinctually, we have this protective barrier around our hearts that immediately go into overdrive during times of duress. Once something is put into overdrive, it takes off like a skyrocket and can only be brought to an end by something powerful or someone with incredible power. If allowed to activate overdrive mode, people with power put into motion what happens with the rest of your life.

The judge that presided over my son's case was allowed to use his power based on the evidence presented to him. I do not deny that my son needed to be punished for his wrongdoing. The bottom line is that when you choose to do wrong regardless of your intellect to do otherwise, you deserve to be punished. With that understood, I do not agree with the forty-year prison sentence that was imposed upon my son when no murder, kidnapping or rape was committed. Though I did not have the power to change his decision to commit a crime, I do have the power to remain my son's keeper.

A fatherless child is like a child being left in the wilderness all alone waiting to be eaten by a bunch of animals. It is painstakingly obvious this exists too often. It is evident simply by going to a school function. There are far too many children unrepresented by their fathers. If more proof were needed of this sad fact, visit a prison. It is filled with fatherless children.

Transitions of life are never easy, but when a young boy does not have his living biological father as his guiding light, something goes astray. His identity seems misplaced as if his father stole it from him when he left his mother. As a result, mothers are left with the daunting task of filling this void. Despite a mother's best efforts, she will barely come close enough to replace the father figure.

Even in prison, my son remains very talented. Before going to prison, he played every sport imaginable and excelled in dance school. Before each game or dance recital, my son's father always made the promise that he would be there. Inevitably, there was always an empty seat, because he never kept his promises. I remember when my son was eleven; he ran the winning touchdown for the team. Amidst the celebration surrounding him, he immediately looked to see his father rejoice but all he saw was an empty seat. It did not matter if myself or his stepfather were there, because this was always the case. He would cling onto the lingering promise of his father in the hope that he would actually be there. When he came off of the field, he always looked so defeated as if he had the life knocked out of him.

Even now, when I visit him in prison, I see that same

empty look in his eyes. Without saying a word, I know he still wonders why his dad does not show up; yet, at the same time, I know he believes it does not really matter because long ago he formed a negative opinion of his father based on all the broken promises. Oddly, I thought when BJ went to prison his dad would visit him especially since he lived in the same state. It has been seven years and, true to form, he continues to be a no-show. I can only imagine the continued disappointment this causes my son, but I also know it's a vicious cycle.

For a son, no one can compare to his biological father. When a father is not present in his son's life, dysfunction rears its ugly face throughout the child's developmental years. Hurt people tend to hurt others and it does not matter who they hurt as long as someone is feeling the same way.

In their early teens, children are very impressionable. Their hormones are raging, and they're trying to figure out so much on their own. They want to live in their youth yet grow into adulthood. They are inquisitive and have so many questions that we cannot always answer. It is also the time for experimentation and seeing how far they can push boundaries. In my heart, I thought all the fighting, giving, sacrificing, and time spent with my son was enough. But maybe it was too much or maybe it was not enough. Somewhere along the way, something went wrong.

If only I could figure out the solution to prevent children from wrongdoings, I could solve one of America's most common problems and the largest decline among children … mass incarceration. Even though I am living through this scenario, I still do not have the wisdom to solve this growing problem.

It has taken a huge amount of courage and determination to remain strong throughout this whole ordeal. No doubt, it is one of the most challenging battles for parents who are going through this to remain their child's keeper. There is an overbearing number of factors involved creating turmoil with each passing moment. The financial aspect alone can send the strongest to their knees begging for mercy. Sometimes all you have left to give is the time you can invest in making sure your incarcerated child has at least one visitor to know all hope is not lost. The visits alone will put you on an emotional rollercoaster that you find yourself riding long after each visit. It is all enough to break down anyone.

Being a mother of four sons, I had always carried a great sense of pride which proved to be one of many strong points; however, during this time, I seemed to be armed more with a sense of inability. I possessed the ability to pray but was incapable to regain my inner peace as my son sat inside the four stone cold walls of a prison cell. For years, I built my own mental jail cell as I suffered in silence. It was during my silence that I also began taking personal responsibility for my son's fundamentally imperfect behavior thereby seemingly validating it.

The hardest part of your child breaking your heart is that your heart never really heals properly. There lives an inner chaos between expectations you always imagine to the actual reality you live. There are too many questions that remain unanswered and a plethora of feelings that remain unchanged. As his mother, despite unforeseen circumstances, I will always choose to remain my son's keeper for as long as I shall live.

November 10, 2011

Ma,

I received the book, <u>Seven Stages of Power and Healing</u>, today. Thank you. I have nothing to do, so I read the book in a matter of hours. Thank you for loving me when I was not always the best. I know that you are the only person *that has my back. I wish I would have listened to you, and I would not be sitting here. I sit behind these four walls with nothing but talent and anger inside. I am so mad at myself. Nobody writes, comes see me, or puts money on my books but you. What would I do without you? I miss you and my brothers so much, Ma. I wish I could go back to being like six years old.*

Lights out, I am about to go to sleep, but I love you and tell my brothers that I love them. See you when you get here next week.

Love BJ

P.S. Please do not forget to put money on my books.

Momma I Should Have Listened

DEAR MOTHERS

"Mothers and their children are in a category all on their own. There's no bond so strong in the entire world. No love so instantaneous and forgiving."
-Gail Tsukiyama, Dreaming Water

If you ask any mother what is most important to her, she will respond with absolute conviction "my children." Where would our children be without their mothers? For most of us, we are the foundation of our households. We are made to push through obstacles without breaking down while continuously trying to make the breakthrough. We are fearless and bold. We are the lifelong cheerleaders. We are made to be strong and build our children with an aptitude for success and without limitations. We are nurturers and heroes. Regardless of what happens in our own lives, we always persevere and move forward. When we are sick, we simply medicate ourselves with no complaint to others. If we have moments of fear or weakness, we go to an area where no one sees us. In that spot, we let out a big sigh, have a cry, stand up, and push through despite never knowing what lies ahead. When our hearts break, and we are engulfed with pain, the only person that truly knows what we are going through is God. Being a mother is the greatest job in the world, but it is also an endless job. Despite all of this, mothers are not perfect.

While mothers inspire dreams and possibilities, there are wounds and misfortunes along the way. No one ever told mothers that such wounds and misfortunes would leave crushed inside suffering massive amounts of pain. No matter the pain, mothers will endure it because of the immense love for our children. Mothers are educators, disciplinarians, confidantes, and best friends to their beloved children. When the unexpected happens, our painful heartbreak runs deeper than any abyss of darkest oceans. The pain of our children will always overshadow the pain of our own past.

As mothers, our duty is to not only hear our children but to listen to them. There will be things we are excited to hear and we celebrate. Unfortunately, there are also things that will bring us to our knees with a sorrowful reality intimidating our souls. Repeatedly, there will be times we must mute our voices even when we have so much to say so we may listen to our children. Our children need to have a voice and, as mothers, we know this is a necessary part of their growth. As much as we try to prevent any pain from harming our children, we are also aware that there will be times we cannot prevent such sorrow. During those times, we must stand firm that God will fix all unimaginable events ... even if we do not bring them to him.

Mothers give life to their children with a love so beautiful there is no scholar that can define it. Mothers can also chip away life with their own thoughts, actions, and ever-changing experiences. In our life shattering moments, we cry rivers. Some of us have been raped, beaten, and brutally broken; yet, we rise. We usually stand in silence, because that is what we are taught. That is what I was taught, anyway. Even now, I can hear my mom in Heaven saying, "What goes on in my house, stays in my house." The excruciating hardships that I encountered in that very house have been tucked away in Pandora's Box never to be discussed again. This is a repeated philosophy.

What happens when we remain silent within ourselves never sharing Pandora's Box with others? We develop an ever-growing sickness that festers and permanently sticks to the depths of our being forever changing our core. Despite our best effort, this sickness never stays locked away forever. It shows its ugly face during our trials and tribulations like some sort of cruel reminder of how bad things can be. What's worse is this cruel sickness passes onto our children, their children, and so on.

As a mother of a son who is spending what should have been the best years of his life in a prison cell, my natural desire is to be there for him by way of visits and making sure that he has what he needs. In an earlier writing, my son mentioned how "we let each other down." This was the hardest thing for me to accept as I had considered myself to be a good mother. Suddenly, I realized that I had actually let him down in ways that my mother had let me down. Like so many of us, we submerse ourselves in our careers dismissing things we consider unimportant. It is later when we realize those "unimportant" things were actually important cries from our children screaming "I need you." It is then our sickness reminds us of that all too familiar feeling of what it feels like to have our cries ignored. Like I said, Pandora's Box is never locked forever.

Our children have no idea what it's like to be a mother. Our first instinct is to work, so we may provide for their needs. Even with the best intentions, we sometimes fail. I can almost hear so many of you mumbling "not me." But it is you. It happens to all of us. There is no such thing as perfect motherhood. Daily, mothers question themselves about their decisions. Was it the right decision? Did I make the right choice? Will there be unknown consequences as a result of such decisions? Mothers tend to parent with guilt when there is no father figure, which turns out to be one of the biggest mistakes that we can ever make.

Most often, when we give tough love in teaching our children life's hard lessons, we are often called mean. In doing our best to help our children grow, we see them distancing themselves from us in defiance. Little do they understand how much they hurt us and bring us to tears. Little do they understand that regardless of our own feelings, we will continue to stand firm for if we don't, we know we will do more harm than good. Children have no clue what it's like to be a mother. The truth is, at their age, we didn't have a clue either.

I do not claim to be a therapist nor a trained professional. I am sharing my own experiences, mistakes, struggles, and triumphs with you in the hope that you will realize you are not alone. You are not the only one going through life's journey. While the path we are on may differ, the journey is filled with much of the same trials and tribulations. We share a common denominator: we are all mothers on the quest to becoming a better parent. One thing that remains true regardless of any circumstances is that a mother's love is a love that never waivers and lives forever.

DEAR STEPPARENTS

We aren't "step", we aren't "half",
we're just family.
-Unknown

While being a parent has many challenges, being a stepparent can hold even more challenges. It is not a role that everyone can handle, so you better be sure you accept all the responsibilities before getting into a relationship. Once you accept the role of stepparent, it is imperative that you embrace the role with courage, understanding, sacrifice, and love. Anything less is unacceptable.

Before my other children were born, my oldest son had a stepparent. Later in my life, my three other children now have a stepparent. They are fortunate to have a wonderful stepparent, and I would not have it any other way. I am a stepparent of three adult children and consider myself a good one. In this chapter, I would like to ask that you understand the capacity of your role as a stepparent. One of the most important things you can do is to understand how a child feels now that you are in his/her life.

My first husband received all of the blame from my oldest son. Whenever disciplinary action was warranted, my son felt like he was the only one receiving it and, to him, the disciplinary measures were harsh. I was torn between my husband and son. There were many accusations, many sleepless nights, and a lot of blame to go around. Compromises and overcompensations made were futile; it was all wrong. My marriage suffered, my family suffered, my son suffered, and my life seemed to slowly unravel. Needless to say, when I finally married again, I firmly decided that if everyone was not on the same plane, the plane would not come off of the runway. Period, end of story.

It is imperative that you put yourself in the child's shoes and walk in them while marinating on the thoughts going through the child's head. You must ask yourself how you would feel if your parents divorced, and you were forced to make a choice as to which parent you wish to live with. Divorce can be really tough for children at any age. Not only do they have to process the divorce, but then there comes a time when one or both parent decides to embark on new relationships. Inevitably, the parent chooses to spend the rest of his/her life with someone else – someone other than their biological parent.

The bottom line is that a child does not have the option to refuse your decision and must accept sharing a future with a person not of his own choice. Take a moment to reflect on that. If you found yourself in this situation, it sure would be tough on you. If there is more than one child, this creates an even bigger dilemma. Take it even further – if there are multiple children and stepchildren. The children do not see each other every day and split their time between two residences. To add fuel to the fire, parents tend to argue constantly about your upbringing rarely agreeing with one another. Each parent has the mentality that "it is my way or the highway." You know who suffers the most, right? That is right - the children. There is an exorbitant amount of emotional and mental imbalances that everyone faces.

The children are not the only ones who feel consequences of this new relationship you have embarked upon. You will go through many emotions as well. You are the person children will blame for breaking up their family even if the home was already broken. No matter how nice you are to them, you may find yourself ignored. It is essential that they like you, because they are part of the package deal with your significant other. It is normal to be on edge, because your life has now been thrown into the hands of a rebellious child who your significant other is catering too because of their own guilt. It is particularly difficult to be told, *"You have to love them like your own,"* when they do not respect you. That being said, you must persevere and understand that this rebellion and disrespect has nothing to do with you. It boils down to neither of you sharing the same DNA, you being an intrusion, and simply an outsider (at least, initially).

It is selfish to believe the notion that a stepparent represents a "bonus friend" to children but not far from the truth. You are the bonus friend that gives their stepchildren great advice, rights the wrongs, provides reasoning in uncomfortable situations between the biological parents, and undoubtedly stands united with them throughout their lives. You are an integral part of the inner circle that will make home so much easier to live in. Just remember not to be that stepparent who speaks negatively about the child's other parent. This never goes over well and merely builds resentment with potential to last a lifetime.

As a stepparent, you will be pushed out of your comfort zone. Your stepchildren are also subject to this, because both of you are on the same journey. Each of you will experience new, and sometimes uncomfortable, feelings. The common denominator is the parent that you both love. You must compromise and be ready to take on the responsibility of what can happen. You will absorb bitterness. You will be disrespected and pushed to your limits. Rather than returning such emotional abuse, walk away and allow your significant other to talk some sense into the child. There is nothing to be gained by arguing or making light of the child's actions. To do so only causes friction and disharmony between the two of you.

You cannot go into a relationship with a person who has children and have unrealistic expectations. If you cannot accept the responsibility or challenges therein, get out of the relationship. Children are not meant to be mistreated, beaten, or harshly criticized by any stepparent (or parent for that matter). Never fail to remember that they did not choose you; it was you that chose to come into their lives by desiring a person that is part of them.

Blended families can be absolutely wonderful. You can create an exceptional relationship built on security, understanding, enjoyment, and unconditional love. If you cannot find it in your heart to love your stepchildren as your own, being a good parent will suffice. The absolute goal is to know what you are getting into before committing to a relationship that you are not willing to accept as a package deal.

DEAR COLORED BOY

"Dream the painting, wake up, and paint the dream."
-Unknown

You are all rebels born for life's greatest moments. Never take for granted your ability to make better decisions than others as being exempt from life's trials and tribulations. You are not untouchable from struggles and challenges. The truth is bad things happen to good people all the time. The ultimate triumph is what we choose to do during bad times. Life changes with every awakening moment. The only promise life makes is that it will come to an end one day. It is up to you to make each day your personal victory.

Regardless of your circumstances, you were created to change the world day by day. To build from a past of brokenness and unexpected diagnosis can be very daunting as you try to forget about stereotypes that society places on you. Society expects you to live curiously and passionately possessing the predisposition that you will know what to do with each day. Many people will try to impress upon you that life is unfair.

The reality is that life is planned in your favor. Your life is channeled by the very choices that you make for yourself. There will be unexpected events and roadblocks that will forcefully move you to detour your path and give up. You must not give in. You must keep driving until the GPS of your intelligence commands you to the exit you should take. Keep in mind the quickest and easiest route is not always the wisest direction and could potentially prove dangerous.

It is likely many of you were raised in families with some sort of adversity. Adversities such as addiction to drugs or gambling, absent fathers, broken homes, alcoholics, parents in prison, abusive parents or maybe you were brought up in foster homes. Regardless, you vehemently strive to make the right decisions. I must apologize for the battles you fight that were handed to you by others. I am thankful for your perseverance and strength in handling some of life's biggest disappointments. I applaud you for appropriately evaluating your life and knowing the right decisions for you avoiding decisions that could negatively impact the rest of your life.

May you recognize that there are things in life that simply cannot be fixed; they can only be carried, meaning everything happens as a result of something else. You have to move forward not by trying to fix what is broken, but rather by carrying the weight of the disappointments with you. The adversities of life are never easy; however, they are reminders that adversity is necessary in leading you exactly where you are meant to be at any given moment. Every adult recognizes the struggle of being a teenager on a quest for manhood. The very quest is more challenging for African American males sustaining the harsh fight against society's cruel stereotypes.

I have written this letter to you to reassure you every dream you have is achievable despite obstacles you may face. In this day of modern technology, everything around you is moving so fast. It is easy to get caught up in the glamorized hype of music videos displaying instant gratification by selling drugs or television shows showing people humiliating themselves for the sake of making quick money. Instant gratification is known as disrespect for time. It creates the "now" mentality. You have this angst of wanting things immediately even if you are not ready for them. There is a time and place for everything. When you receive things with no regard to proper timing, it can become uncomfortable and painful in the long run.

You cannot create anything without spending a considerable amount of time mastering the required skills to fulfill such creation. Do not get caught up in the carefully crafted fortune and fame. Music videos show rappers throwing money in the air as if to suggest rapping will instantly make you rich overflowing with cash. In actuality, that very money is picked up and thrown a thousand more times to get the shot just right before final production is in place. It was a premeditated idea meant to delve into your dreams to convince you that you too can rapidly be rolling in cash.

You must be wise enough to realize that everything in the video was planned and directed. It is not common reality. The reality is that you must do the hard work and earn the place you wish to see yourself. To be clear, if even for a moment you believe fame and fortune will come quickly by stealing, selling drugs, committing robberies, or any myriad of other mistaken behaviors, you can easily find yourself in the space of a prison cell - mental or physical. Overnight success does not exist.

We presently live in what I refer to as "microwave" times where information is instantly transformed through the quick click of a button. We all are privy to the same information by technology. The affluence that technology brings bridges the gap between the rich and the poor. Everything has such an intense sense of urgency, but we all know Noah did not build the ark in a day. Quite frankly, anything that comes too fast is usually riddled in risk and falsehood.

This letter is not meant to preach to you. It is meant to scare you into being a better individual despite some of the calamities that you may face. One of the worst heartaches you can give to your parents would be choosing the Road of Destruction. With all its grand promises and too-good-to-be-true notions, you will only find yourself being led to Prison Avenue or Death Lane.

Sons, I know that life is not easy. Contrary to what you may believe, we as parents recognize that, because we were once in your very shoes. We know that there will be disruptions in your lives. Our biggest prayer is that you strive hard to eliminate such disruptions with everything in you while taking God's positive antidotes and moving forward. The greatest pain that a parent can endure is to lose his/her child to the prison system or to the graveyard.

Your parent(s) chose life for you with the hope that you would respect your life even when troubles arise. You have no reason not to honor the gifts living inside of you. Your light should never dim, and you should never devalue the man that lives within you. You cannot be influenced by a curse of generations. Break those chains! We all have inherited traits that we can use as an excuse for making bad choices, but the better solution is to take the high road - your own perfectly chosen road on your own terms with no thought whatsoever to resort to genetic excuses for your choices.

When you are handed lemons, make lemonade. Like life, the world is wondering what you are going to do with it especially when you must become your own hero. Put education, respect, dreams, goals and hard work on your trials and tribulations. Make life for you with no regard for who is in your corner. It is your choice, your life. You will never be armed with personal cheerleaders. Be your own cheerleader; your own hero. Overcome disappointments by being your own cheerleader. Your inner hero is begging for your attention at all times.

I applaud you for not giving into the stereotypes that society solicits upon you. I believe in your life! I believe in your vision and, most of all, I believe in the path you are taking to make your purpose come to full fruition. I implore you to believe in your curiosity and inquisitive thoughts allowing your internal motivation to take your dreams and turn them into your reality.

As a mother whose son is living life in the prison system, but also a mother of three other sons, I empathize with what it is like to be a black male in today's world. Beyond a shadow of a doubt, I know that with hard work and determination, you can overcome the stigmata others may place upon you. Not only are you fighting for your place in society, but you are also fighting to please the people who matter most to you whether it is your family, teachers, friends or even gangs.

Children tend to join gangs to be an accepted outcast; however, you are only placing yourself in a position to become susceptible to unfamiliar territory. You begin making poor decisions that result in the onslaught of bad recreation. The negative abyss of that makes it nearly impossible to redeem yourself when you come to the realization that you must change. You need to understand that no one is entitled to have what they want precisely when they want it. There are rules and guidelines set in place throughout your lifeline to follow. If these are not followed in the free world, you will find yourself following them in the inhumane world of a prison system.

You must ask yourself a very important question: Do you want to trust the sometimes-uncomfortable guidance of your parents, or do you want to leave to find your own way? While under the guidance of your parents, there will be times when you do not agree with their decisions for you even though their life experiences become easy lessons for you. In other words, they have already gone through the hard part in learning the lessons. They teach you these lessons in the hope you are not burdened by the learning curve. Do you trust being uncomfortable now while learning, or do you go out on your own, which may lead to uncomfortable consequences affecting the rest of your life? The choice is yours. My message is to open your eyes to the bigger picture to help you understand that today's decision is tomorrow's reality and, unfortunately, the consequences of your decisions cannot be changed, revoked or reversed.

Every choice you make has a result, good or bad. With maturity comes growth. With growth comes knowledge and wisdom. If I could teach you only one thing in this very moment, I would teach you to be patient and broaden your perspective to see that life has so much more to offer you than you are able to see right now. Trust the process of growth and the teachings of your elders. They want the best for you.

BJ's Mom

COLLATERAL DAMAGE

"Don't think or judge, just listen."
-Sarah Dessen, Just Listen

Last night, I was watching the news about a man whose son was accused of murdering a child. After leaving the arraignment, the father of the accuser was questioned by news reporters. They asked, "Do you think your son did this?" Even though all hands pointed to his teenage son who was once a star athlete, the man had a mini breakdown and said, "No." Because this was being played out in the media, people seemed all too eager to stand in judgment never knowing the facts. It is considered normal; a child was killed, and his son was accused of being the murderer. Nobody cares. People think, "Thank you for your imperfect parenting skills and not reading your parental manual before having this kid who is now a murderer!"

Anytime we learn that our children have done something of poor judgement, or are in the process of going down "wrong" street, our immediate reaction is to say, "Not my child." For more reasons than one, I hurt for this man on the news when I saw his breakdown. So many people would question my ability to feel for this father when his son is the accused killer. Let me explain how I can feel for this man's heartbreak.

I have been there. I do not feel sorry for this man's child; I empathize with the father. While he did not commit the crime, his life was shattered in an instant when his son was convicted. This is usually, but not always, the first stage of grief. I understood wholeheartedly his initial response especially when his son had not been in trouble before. As all parents do, we rationalize our feelings while thinking, "How could this be happening and why?" When you are going through the legal process, and without even having to try, you block out your feelings. You do not even consider the facts until they are actually confessed to you. You try to convince yourself the crime was never committed and certainly not by your own beloved child.

Then there is the natural progression of other questions. Does anyone honestly believe this man wanted to believe his son murdered anyone let alone a child that could not defend himself? How will the public view him as a parent? What will become of his precious son? Where did he go wrong in being a role model for this child? Did his child not know right from wrong? Why? Why? Why?

You become overwhelmed with feelings of helplessness and any hope you had fades away in the far distance. In the face of another people's blame against you, you begin to question yourself. You start to lose control of your own feelings, because you are too busy worrying about what you have to do next to make all of it go away.

Like many, judgment was the answer to every aspect of my life. I would pick up the newspaper or look at the news, and the first thing I would think was, "Yep, the parents are definitely at fault." I could never connect or understand those parents, because I was certain it would never happen in my family. I was positive those parents were at fault. I was also positive that whatever happened to them and their children was exactly as it should be ... no exceptions. I was so judgmental in thinking their children acted as they did because of misguidance from their parents. Questions came as easy as the breeze on a wintry day. "Where are their parents?" "If they were good parents, this would have never happened." "What kind of upbringing did they have that led them down the wrong path?"

We never think about the reverse side of things. That is until we are on the receiving side. When my son got incarcerated, I immediately changed my previous judgmental thinking. That happens when you find yourself in the shoes of another person. Whenever our children make poor decisions, it is understood that those poor decisions are not ours as parents. Yet, when our children are successful, we tend to assume that success is a direct result of our superior parenting. You commonly hear, "Wow, your children are great, and that says a lot about you." We love to hear that. It is ironic that their failures are the fault of someone or something else; however, their successes are surely a result of being terrific parents.

I became angry all over again at his father. BJ would run to him, cry out for him, and love him when he really did not know him. I was the one who comforted him, parented in guilt, overcompensated, and humbled my feelings of rage when I was outraged. Neither of us ever had much contact with his father that was not negative. BJ started having contact with his father when he was about thirteen years old, which is a very impressionable age; hence, this is when the problems began.

When one parent is raising their child without help from the other parent, it is easy to place blame on that other parent. It was not until I realized the pain and brokenness that his father had experienced that my anger started to lessen. Until writing this chapter, I had always placed blame on his father saying things like, "He was not a father figure." "Children need their fathers, especially boys." "His father was a career criminal." All of these statements allowed me to survive my own parental uncertainty. It was easier to place blame on his father, because it distracted me of thinking my child could be capable of any criminal behavior.

The mother of Dylan Keibold, one of the Columbine shooters, had no idea that her son would leave home that morning and shoot up the high school. If she had any suspicion whatsoever, there is no doubt she would have done everything to intercept his intentions that fateful day.

We fall into a place of thinking we failed them. In some instances, it is true. While many factors come into play, my failure as a parent is not one of them. By no means was I ever a perfect parent. I have always done my best to lead by example by working hard, demonstrating a strong foundation, and encouraging my children to have morals and principals. My son's choices were just that - his choices. One thought that never escapes my mind is that had I been less oblivious of his first bad choice, maybe I could have prevented future bad choices.

HEALED BY TIME

"Sometimes it's the same moments that take your breath away that breathe purpose and love back into your life."
-Steve Maraboli, Unapologetically You

You have a personal view into my pain, frustration, and what my life was like for so long even when it seemed nearly perfect. Regardless of life's tragedies, trials, and tribulations, you must always believe. No matter how many scars we bear, there will always be opportunities that God places before us as a reminder that life has been prepared in our favor.

Fast forward to August 12, 2015 - my plane has touched down in New Orleans after attending the *Straight Outta Compton* movie premiere in Los Angeles. It was such an amazing, beautiful, and rewarding night! What made the night such a rewarding experience is that I found myself walking on the red carpet under the most luminescent lighting next to someone who reminded me so much of my son. His life once resembled that of my son, but he chose to make the best out of it when so many doubted him.

I was proud to be a contributing factor as the developmental agent to Jason Mitchell who always had a dream of becoming an actor. His dream came true when he was casted as one of the lead actors in the *Straight Outta Compton* film. He was chosen to portray the infamous Eazy-E, a West Coast rapper and label co-founder who was part of the group N.W.A. With everything that I had been going through, and the multiple times I almost gave up, God made it known that He was not finished with my journey yet. The blood, sweat, and tears were all in preparation for this very night and this very moment that I now stood in. I was truly humbled, proud, and honored.

Looking back six years, I realize that I was so vulnerable, ashamed, broken, and embarrassed of my life. Despite my high self-esteem, I was ready to let go. It was only through the power of God and my own perseverance that I hung on all the while rebuilding my inner strength and being. When you feel ashamed, embarrassed, and are hiding something damaging that is going on in your life, it is in that very moment you need life support the most. To the outside world, I effortlessly presented an illusion of myself with my vivacious smile, astute attitude, and invulnerable nature. The outside world never saw the near-dead person inside of me wanting to be carried away from the life support that was simply functioning day-to-day.

From my beautiful mom passing away and then my son's imprisonment, the despair overwhelmed me and became the essence of who I had become. The gut wrenching moments I was experiencing were so deeply personal, yet seemed so minimal to the people around me. Superficially, my friends (that I now paraphrase as associates) were uselessly hanging onto my continuous battle with severe depression. The more depressed I became, the more vulnerable I became to those very people who desired to take advantage of it. When you're going through a detrimental time in your life, it is then that the perpetrators acknowledge your misfortunes. Perpetrators tend to be the people who are closest to you. They understand that the core of your soul is resisting internally against who you are portraying externally. With deliberate moves, these perpetrators will eat you alive with their own propaganda like lions ravaging prey.

Watching my son sit behind a jail cell has taught me so much. Though this experience had to break me first, it also healed me in innumerable ways. Throughout my healing process, I have learned not to judge anyone, to embrace human error, and that we must all go through self-discovery. I have also learned to have mercy on the souls of my frenemies and to disconnect from a world of expectations. For me, expectations created problems that almost destroyed me. When you have expectations of those you love and those expectations do not come to fruition, you must inherently learn to accept non-expectations. For instance, if you have a child that is homosexual or mentally challenged, your first inclination is not to accept it, because you did not expect it. This is how I felt about my son who robbed people of their prized possessions, but I was forced to accept his shortcomings as a result of me choosing to love him unconditionally.

I chose to love my son who, despite having a heart of gold, was vulnerable, a follower, and lived through the life of his father. It is human nature to expect everything in our lives to turn out perfectly; however, the reality is that perfection is nearly impossible. As parents, we operate in this disposition and when things do not work as we expect, we turn our backs and hope the problem is rehabilitated on its own. Though some things are out of our control, there are certain things that can be limited within our control.

Many nights I blamed myself for the mistakes my son made. I was criticized by others for not being hard enough on him or for giving him too much of what his heart desired. As any parent can attest, there is no manual for parenting ... or life, for that matter. All of our lessons come from our experiences and sometimes experience is a lifelong learning process. Like anything in life, the first time is always a challenge and likely the hardest. As my grandmother would say, "I hope you do not pay dearly for your mistakes." Unfortunately, my son is paying for his mistakes with a forty-year sentence.

I have properly and critically evaluated the true meaning of my journey. My journey was never set to be normal; my journey was set to live proudly and authentically through the experiences and challenges that God has set aside for me. My pain turned into headaches, my headaches turned into heartaches, and my severe bouts of depression and suicide attempts were my challenges to overcome. I now accept those challenges as a proud, brave, and courageous woman. I accept my son's forty-year journey not with a fight of being right or wrong, but a fight of injustice of time.

Writing this book has been filled with a rollercoaster of emotions, yet also been such a miraculous journey. I learned the facts, endured many truths, bonded with my son through his writings, and, most importantly, I allowed myself to feel every single precious moment of it. I allowed my heart to break in many pieces over and over again. With each chapter, I have come to learn who I was, who I am, and who I am becoming. I embrace the power I hold from within, which lives through every moment of every day. I have come to know the true meaning of unconditional love. My past mindset is now healed by the experiences God chose for me.

Only time could restore what I had lost, which was the transformative power of gratitude, optimism, and happiness. Today, I manage my weaknesses and master my strengths. I was broken, but now I am healed. I accept that I have to be on this journey with my son for the next thirty-three years. The unwavering truth that has remained constant throughout all of this is the love that I, as a mother, have for my son.

I hear my son clearly when he tells me that he finally understands. He acknowledges that he should have listened. He has come to realize that those friends and family who were there during times of conflict and angst are no longer there for him during his time of hardship and despair. He has truly come to understand that out of sight means out of mind. In his words …

MOMMA I SHOULD HAVE LISTENED

Living in a world colder than North Boston
Momma eyes see more water than sink faucets
Hated that I treated you like that
One in a million like Aliyah, hated to see you like that
So many crazy nights, unorthodox life
Just wanted to be next to the father I looked just like
So asking why he don't love me, I am his first born
Ashamed to be with me like I lost both arms
Like my face was disfigured or had cross eyes
And I was deaf or missing an ear on one side
Love was unbalanced and feelings wasn't mutual
Me being a part of his world wasn't doable
But you told me there was going to be emotional harm
He was doing you wrong before I was even born
And me being a kid I didn't realize the dynamics
Didn't understand you were trying to keep me away
from the damage
I felt since you hated him, you wanted me to hate him
too
And since you started to keep me away from someone I
love
I started disliking you
And I really felt like this is some stupid it
You hate my dad, but not your ex-husband's abusiveness
So it was very hard to listen to wisdom I wasn't wise at
that age
That was like telling a blind man to look both ways
So I hated to be under the same roof, I didn't feel
comfortable there
So everywhere I went, I was trying to get comfortable
there

Running away from home little crazy me
Did not have anywhere to go but the streets
And that was a whole other lifestyle at its best
The streets will make you think they love you, but can
really care less
And under my circumstances I was the easiest victim
The DA was like "It's going to be easy to convict him"
And now I feel stupid because I had several warnings
Now I am waking up to prison trays every morning
No sympathy for a dysfunctional family
Seventeen year old mother and an absent daddy
Abusive stepfather who I disliked to the core
And he knew it so he messed over me even more
But in everyone eyes I was the bad news
Not considering that I was emotionally confused
But none of that matter that still don't justify
Why me and my crew were robbing and hurting lives
As a teenager I should have been in school
Instead I was breaking the law like a damn fool
I've changed now but with a forty year sentence
And I admit MOMMA, I SHOULD HAVE LISTENED

THE END

AUTHOR'S NOTE

Milan

"Tears are words that need to be written."
-Paul Coelho

While reading Facebook this morning, I came across a post by a woman who was approaching the second anniversary of her only daughter's death. Imani Ruffins's daughter, Milan, was young, smart, and beautiful. Her life was tragically ended by the senseless act of gun violence. What touched me more than the pain she expressed was the haunting place that the very navigated your soul into. It was what I envisioned for myself.

Her heartfelt descriptive words put readers in her shoes and did so with such poignant grace. This was not the first time that I read a post by Imani Ruffin. I read other posts she wrote about missing her daughter and the pain that she constantly felt, but this one was different. I have always empathized with her and, quite frankly, felt like our lives were parallel to one another. Same struggles; different circumstances.

As I continued reading her post, my heart pounded louder with each beat and tears poured from my eyes like flood gates had been opened. The hall she walked down in the hospital was similar to the hall I still see myself walking down on the afternoon of September 9, 2009 at the Harris County Court. Both halls were cold, eerie, and seemed to be never-ending. While my walk was full of shame, embarrassment, disgrace, and vexation, Imani's walk lingered with unimaginable torture.

Though our walks were vastly different, they were identical in that they were both instances of collateral damage. It was the finalities of those walks that were similar. Each represented the final stage of a struggle that one would never imagine living through. I could not help but think of the state of mind she was in while writing her heartfelt post all while carrying the legacy of her daughter. With Imani's permission, these are her words verbatim:

I read an article last year in relation to a lady who lost her husband to cancer. She referenced the anniversary of his death as getting on a train every year. This is my version of THAT TRAIN.

It'll be two years without Milan and all I can think about is next month.

2 whole years?

An Anniversary?

Anniversaries are to be celebrated. Milan getting shot in the back and killed is NOT a celebration.

The anniversary train is coming! I know it's arriving; it's coming July 3, 2017, on schedule.

And I'm supposed to get on it?

Ride that train for the day?

Ride its heaviness?

It takes forever to get to the destination.

Except it never really stops, because I live it

EVERYDAY. it's never over!

It is not her birthday.

It is her death day.

Every time someone ask "what are you
doing for the anniversary of Milan?" I get
nauseous. All those thoughts from "that
day". The phone call. The drive from Baton
Rouge. The walk to the hospital's entrance.
All the police officers standing out front. My
family sitting in a private room to the left.
All the strangers sitting in the emergency
room to right.

I already knew.

I remember how many times I asked to see
my baby. I remember telling them "she's
alone. I need to see her. and she needs me by
her side". I remember pacing back and forth
for what seemed like hours.

I remember screaming so loud that it caused
me to black out (I assume) because several

times I remember multiple people on top of me trying to restrain me.

I remember the Dr. coming in to give us "the speech". I remember looking at my family's faces, everyone was crying, it was in slow motion, but I was calm. I remember standing calmly asking to see her.

I remember me and my brother Lloyd walking that hallway, it was so long. I remember my two co-workers, my two friends, two homicide detectives, standing in that room when I entered. I walked to Milan's bedside.

My baby. My first child, my only daughter, my best friend, Milan, laying there. Still. At peace.

I remember a white sheet covered her from the neck down. Her face was clean, not a hair out of place. My first instinct was to climb in bed with her but I knew it would put me in an emotional state that I would never recover from.

I leaned over and kissed her. I began saying the Our Father Prayer, aloud. I said "I love you Milan" and in that moment it was real, Milan was dead. My heart was broken, Imani was dead, with Milan.

I remember leaving that hospital, head forward not making eye contact with a single person. My only concerns were how do I tell Zavier?

I remember calling her dad a thousand times but to no avail. He was on vacation in another country. Could this be any worse?

I don't want to celebrate "that day."

Social Media has been my platform to express my inner most thoughts and allowed me to share Milan's life. For that I'm grateful.

But I don't want to get on THAT train. It is not going to bring me to Milan.

Milan is in me. She's in my memories.

I'll wait until August 27, 2017, her 23 birthday to celebrate her life.

I MISS THIS CHILD WITH EVERYTHING IN MY SOUL. Which is why I will forever be "SOUL-LESS." #milanslifematters

---

I was touched so much by her post that I reached out to her. As much as I was familiar with her story, I wanted to know more about her daughter. I wanted to hear her words in her voice about the character of her daughter. I wanted to give her the moment to speak to a stranger, another woman, a mother who had experienced loss but a different kind of loss. Listening to Imani speak so eloquently about Milan, her best friend, her only daughter, a daughter that she asked God for, her oldest child who was an honor student destined for greatness, was refreshing and breathtaking. The strength she displayed was a symbol of sitting in that train station.

The stillness of the emotions is the train station. It is stationary, permanent, and it allows her to feel and remember. It is her serenity for Milan. As a mother, I am connected to her emotions. While speaking with Imani, my tears came from a multitude of places. One of those places was remembering how hard it was to navigate the transition after experiencing such a major loss, especially the loss of a child. She feels that if she moves from her seat at the train station to get on the next moving train then the legacy of her daughter will no longer live. I understood this notion. I get it! Personal tragedies will either thrust you forward or cause you to stay trapped repeating the past over and over again.

What I wanted from Imani more than anything was for her to transition her pain into power. As parents, we want our kids to be great. We want to know when they leave that they will be back. I want Imani to get on that next train in the memory of Milan, so she can create awareness and empower mothers like us. In doing so, Milan's legacy lives, and everyone will know her story. When others learn what you have gone through, they can begin to realize that, like you, they too can pull through almost anything. While we may never get over times like this, we can find some peace in knowing we will be able to edge our way around it.

Can we save the world? Absolutely not; however, this book and the aforementioned feelings of another mother should empower you to start a movement that can possibly save one third of it.

Allow Imani's infamous hashtag, #milanslifematters, to really matter. It is time for all of us to get on that moving train and move forward for the future of this generation and generations to follow. The initiative must start at some point in time and that time is now.

ABOUT THE AUTHOR

Tosha Smith Mills is an entrepreneur with over fifteen years as CEO of The Talent Connexion, LLC, a successful talent agency in New Orleans, who has placed talent in an extensive list of Hollywood accredited films, television shows, and commercials; Tosha also has over eighteen years of experience in the legal field. Through this, she has discovered her passion in writing and is fulfilled by sharing her testimonies, empowering those in need, and helping others find their life's purpose.

Tosha is a native New Orleanian and is the wife to John, a mother to four young men, Blake, William, Christopher, and Trae, and a source of inspiration to all.